1968

LOVE and the PERSON

Maurice Nédoncelle

LOVE AND THE PERSON

TRANSLATED BY *Sr. Ruth Adelaide, S.C.*

Sheed & Ward ◊ *New York*

© Sheed and Ward, Inc., 1966

Originally published in French under the title Vers Une Philosophie de l'Amour et de la Personne, © 1957, Aubier Editions Montaigne, Paris.

Library of Congress Catalog Number 66-22019

Nihil obstat:
  Thomas J. Beary
  Censor Librorum

Imprimatur:
  † Robert F. Joyce
  Bishop of Burlington
  June 30, 1966

Manufactured in the United States of America

Translator's Note

Translating Maurice Nédoncelle's *Vers une philosophie de l'amour et de la personne* has been a difficult pleasure—a fact that should surprise no one who has read this French philosopher in the original. I only hope the pleasure is more apparent than the difficulty.

The reader should be informed, however, of at least one of the translator's problems and her attempted solution to it. It involves an expression that is not only central to Nédoncelle's philosophy but also characteristic of his use of language: *réciprocité des consciences*. The author rarely uses the word *conscience* as "conscience" in the moral sense but almost always as "consciousness"—not merely as "awareness," but pushed to the limits of the notion of "person" as a unique existent. This much is clear from the context. A difficulty arises for the translator, however, when *conscience* occurs in the plural, as in *réciprocité des consciences*. Anyone who has seen the plural of the English word "consciousness" in print and tried it for sound will understand why one would look for a substitute. Rev. Vincent T. Liddle, C.M., looked for one when preparing his doctoral dissertation, "The Ethical Implications of the Philosophy of Maurice Nédoncelle" (Louvain, 1965). He finally selected "centers of consciousness" as an alternative for "consciousnesses." With the approval of Canon Nédoncelle—who is also an English scholar—I, too, have used this formula in most instances where *consciences* occurs in the French.

While responsibility for defects in this translation is to be laid at my door alone, any merits it may have are partly due to the suggestions of Sister Julia Marie, S.C., who read the original draft, and to Rev. Henry J. Miron and Mr. Thomas L. Seibert, who scrutinized parts of it with meticulous care. Gratitude is due in particular, however, to Canon Nédoncelle himself, who carefully read, annotated, and approved the translation in its final form.

—S.R.A.

Preface

Interpersonal philosophy was not yet in style in 1942 when this author wrote *La réciprocité des consciences*. Therefore he was persuaded to explain its principles, as he conceived them, for a larger public than the one composed of his regular readers. This was the origin of a lecture on love, given in Paris in 1944, under the auspices of the late Paul Archambault. The author's thesis was in contrast with the then recent studies of Nygren and Sartre. This lecture was enlarged and published in 1946 under the title: *Vers une philosophie de l'amour*.

Many years have since elapsed. In re-editing my sketch today I integrated it into a single whole, with the result that a book twice the size of the original work has come off the press. The title itself has been somewhat modified to show the link between the problem of love and the problem of the person, for one of the leading ideas of this study is that love proceeds from persons and is directed toward them. When love takes other forms it is incomplete and still seeking its true identity.

The earlier essay constitutes the first part of this book. The original theme is then prolonged in two directions. On the one hand I examine some aspects of the mysterious continuity that can unite centers of consciousness without destroying their individuality. On the other I try to show the limits of this continuity in private life and in group relations. By way of conclusion, a synthesis brings together the principal affirmations not only of this work but also of other essays I have devoted to the philosophy of the person.

All these changes notwithstanding, the volume is not a treatise. It is still a collection of essays. It retains the purpose of the study of 1946, since it can serve now, even better than it did then, as an introduction to several other works which it prepares or summarizes, clarifies or complements, and occasionally even supplements. It does not depart, however, from a central inquiry concerning the *I-thou* relationship. This must be emphasized. Fascinating and lengthy analyses in inter-individual psychology or microsociology are certainly not lacking. But the philosophy called for by such studies is almost constantly neglected. It is surprising that so many authors leap right over the problems of intersubjective causality and the perception of the other as if they did not see any problem or—what is worse—as if they were in possession of evident and adequate solutions to it.

A philosophical introduction ought to seize ideas from above. It follows that in these pages love and person are rather often studied in their principles and not in their particular situations in the family, friendship, professions, etc. I do not think excessive abstraction or premature generalization results. It is possible to reach the real in the common elements of experience as well as in a series of divergent details. But perhaps I ought to warn of a danger of another kind, especially for young readers. Dealing with pure essence does not speed the journey. Though perfection may be immediately glimpsed, it is never given completely, all at once, and ready-made; it must be courageously and painfully won; it supports from above an existence that gropes its way until death.

Aristotle used to say: "My friends, there is no friend. . . ." Did he mean that to have several friends is to have none? Or that all friendship is illusory? It is a bitter statement, and if the quip were a theorem, the theorem would be false. But it is true that we are always at a distance from the love that is addressed to the person or, if one prefers, from the person who responds totally to the exigency of love. Likewise it would be contrary to my purpose were I to belittle, under pretext of extracting a pure essence, the institutional order wherein men have often given proof of experience and wisdom that cannot be neglected with impunity. In these two respects a metaphysics of escape or facility would do no service to life, although life reveals its secret only at the metaphysical level where it concentrates upon and transcends itself.

To conclude, it is proper to deliberately use the word metaphysics and not phenomenology only. For it is proper to an inquiry on person not to dissociate these two kinds of research for any length of time. The present effort will lead neither to a radical separation of description from reflection nor to a confusion of the two. The origin and destiny of beings in general is seen up to a certain point in the experience of each rational being that does not cheapen its experience by yielding to overconfidence or despair, but tries to determine its essential constancy and fundamental relations.[1]

NOTES

1. I am grateful to the various publishers who have allowed me to use certain articles appearing under their auspices. The following are the items in question and the periodicals or collections where they were published, at least in part. For chapter 4, the *Giornale di Metafisica*, Vol. V, Jan.–Feb. 1950; chapter 5: the *Actes du Congrès international de philosophie* of Amsterdam, 1948; chapter 6: the *Actes du Congrès des Sociétés de philosophie de langue française* of Neuchâtel, 1949. For chapters 9–11: the *Actes des Congrès de philosophie de langue française*, Aix-en-Provence (1957), Strasbourg (1952), Grenoble (1954); chapter 12, the *Revue des sciences religieuses*, Vol. XXIX, May–October, 1949. Finally, for the conclusion: *L'Encyclopédie française*, Vol. XIX.

Contents

xi

LOVE and the
PERSON

I ⬥ Concerning Love

To know the strange diversity of human relations one has only to watch briefly the passersby on a busy street. One person avoids men and remains a stranger to his fellows. Another challenges them and delights in the strategies of competition and conflict. Still another loves them and advances eagerly to an encounter with friends. . . .

Each time a person consciously relates to another, a complete system is formed, having its own end and means. It is like a world within the world, a sphere of countless attitudes that, for all its originality, can communicate with other conscious spheres. In the presence of others we pass at each moment from one of these worlds to another; we create or repeat a variation of relationship that immediately rearranges the whole chain of our personal associations. Every glance has the power to transform our outlook; with each new encounter the network of interdependent minds, cast together in the adventure of existence, is unraveled and woven together again into a new design. We shape our own destinies in the progressive, radiating moments of time; we change

5

ourselves with our changing social vision; and society itself changes in the play of interpersonal glances.

Let us examine love, one of these spheres of personal encounter. We soon discover that it contains a thousand kingdoms that at first overwhelm us by their variety and number. Here is a couple walking arm in arm in ecstasy; this, certainly, is the way of lovers and, presumably, a loving state of soul. But here is a mother cradling her child and this, too, is love. And there is a youth leading his little brother by the hand, ready to defend him from a bully's brutality; and this, too, is love. The handclasp I exchange with my friend, the coin I drop in the blind man's cup, the bittersweet generosity of hidden self-sacrifice . . . what a multitude of forms love takes! Protective strength and timid sensitivity, the frank exchange of a common gift, the tears that beg pardon and the ones that forgive, the visit to the sick man, Hermione's wrath and Abraham's poised blade—one thing only is common to them all: the love that evoked them.

Because the philosopher must first determine the psychologic essence of love, we shall begin by trying to isolate that unique element that is at once diffused and hidden in the species and occasionally bestirs itself to produce strange and agonizing metamorphoses. What is the nature of the love at the heart of all loves?

Furthermore, accompanying the interior attitude there is always an expression and a task. The person who loves gives at least his thoughts to the beloved; and into their stream he often casts the force of moral and material influence; he aids the beloved, and by so doing affirms his own will. If the sentiment is a reciprocal and a happy one, a common work seals the union.

Our second problem, then, is to determine the characteristics of the loving work and its relation to the loving intent.

Finally, because love pursues value and is itself a value, we must examine the fundamental consistency and dignity of love to determine its level in the realm of the ideal and its rightful place in reality.

1 ✧ *The Essence of Love*

A WILL TO PROMOTION

Among all the concepts attached to a given word we should choose the most authentic one, the one that can help us understand even the anomalies, twists and distortions to which the word is liable. Now, the concept that satisfies these requirements and that should enter into the definition we are looking for is the following: love is a will to promotion. The *I* that loves is willing above all the existence of the *thou;* it subsequently wills the autonomous development of the *thou;* and finally wills that this autonomous development be, if possible, in harmony with the value the *I* anticipates for the *thou.* Any other desire would be either a timid hesitation on the threshold of the temple or egoistic delight in a mirrored reflection. There is no love properly so-called unless there are two, and unless the *I* undertakes to go out to the *thou* in order to regard him in the truest possible sense, not as an object of curiosity, but as an interior existence having perfect subjectivity.

Max Scheler defined love in a way that coincides partly

8

with our proposal but ultimately differs from it. According to him, love is an intentional movement causing a superior value to appear in a concrete being. It is never motivated by the knowledge of a value that that being may have already acquired in its empiric existence. Thus one can love a criminal as well as a saint: in both cases the lover rises toward an excellence inherent in the one of whom he is enamored; and this excellence subsists in the realm of value no matter what may have been the conduct of the loved one up to this time. But what is the object of love? It may be three-fold: I can become attached to the vital being of the other, and the highest value I see in him—the exaltation of sexuality for example—becomes the nobility of his being. I can place myself on a higher level and love the psychic reality of the other; this new orientation will lead me to values of culture and truth. Finally, at the highest level, it is his spiritual nature that enthralls me, and the value I then perceive is the very person of the other. Only personal love is moral; here the good is not extrinsic to the *thou,* it is the *thou* itself.[1]

There is much to be retained from this analysis. But Scheler adds certain refinements to his thesis that make it very debatable. In love, as he sees it, there is never anything to be accomplished. "What," he asks, "can a mother really will as she lovingly contemplates her sleeping child?" Certainly, the active, educative attitude may be a consequence of love, but it would not be essential to love itself. It is, in effect, impossible for Scheler to insert the will into love, for according to him, the will is purely executive in character; it is devoid of any intentionality or direction of its own.

I fear that his decision to limit love to an emotional contemplation is a grave error. If we separate sentiment and self-sacrifice at the base of love, love itself is destroyed. The primordial drive of the self is not only an impulse toward the other and toward the inner value of the other, as Scheler so admirably showed; it is also an efficient energy that wants to contribute to the existence and development of the other. Thus it is not a question of directing him toward some extrinsic end nor of using him as a means for the triumph of a value foreign to his unique vocation. It is a question of giving him the solidity and perfection of his singular personality and striving for the boundless liberty of his unfettered being. Love is not a lazy repose in the beauty of an image, but a vital involvement, a vigorous commitment, a straining toward the fulfillment of the *thou.* Even in contemplation there should be an active desire.[2]

Does this mean that the will to advancement is a will to creation? Perhaps. In principle, the lover longs to engender wholly the being of the beloved. However, a human person cannot, in fact, pretend to such a thing. We try to consolidate the existence of the *thou* or contribute to his growth. But we always fall short at some point. Often our control goes no farther than our imagination, as in the case of the novelist who brings his characters to life on paper; sometimes he manages to stammer out a new essence but his phantoms evolve in a misty existence, powerless to come fully alive. We give a child bread to help his physical growth; we may come to the assistance of a friend, influence a mind and modify its qualities. But man does not create man.

Someone will object, saying that he procreates him. Is this truly an objection? On this point I find myself again in agreement with Scheler: procreation is not a relation of spiritual causality. There is no direct continuity between the parents and the soul of their child. The *ingenium* of the son descends from heaven to earth. To the degree that the son is himself he is not hereditary; he is not proportionate to the paternal *ingenium*. His arrival is basically independent of the designs of the parents. The sex act is subjectively the expression of conjugal affection and implies in itself nothing more in this respect. The fact that conception may take place without any thought being directed to the possibility of offspring should suffice to show up the weakness of the alleged creative powers of the procreators. Conjugal love may indeed include the desire for the child and penetrate the sex act with an intention it did not originally have. The moralist will be generous with good advice on this subject. But the fact remains that the arrival of the child is always a gift and a surprise. What is hereditary is not owing to the will of the parents; it is only the resemblances of repetitious qualities that are transmitted from one generation to the next.

Now, a child is something other than a mass of qualities, he is a new germ of personality who will have to make his own choice from among the totality of traits to which he is liable and integrate them little by little according to an unforeseeable design. Strictly from the viewpoint of causality, which supposes a conscious will to advancement, influence cannot begin unless the child is already there. We never create another personality, we discover it. Between it and us there is an initial gulf that cannot be crossed. In the geometry of souls the lines are at first parallel; only later do destinies touch and intersect.

Wise old Plato was right on this point. He maintained

that in our human experience love originates in the loveableness of the beloved. We receive the beloved, we discover in him reasons for cherishing him even if he be vile or vilified. The stream of love then flows from the beloved to the lover and back again, enriched in its content and intensified in its movement. But Plato, I will admit, does not take into sufficient account the gratuitous initiative of the lover—an initiative proportionate to the nobility of his love. Even though love may be rooted in necessity it flowers in freedom; it is perception, but it is also creative imagination; the autonomy love would give, it first acquires itself; and if, to some extent, it always receives what it gives, it is simply to learn to give more and more while receiving less and less. The very act of receiving tends to be the result of a conscious work; the act is experienced in order to be confirmed; and from then on it is willed.

If the lover is not entirely the creator, must we conclude that he means to withdraw for the greater good of the *thou* and that this good is realized only by his retreat? This extreme does not necessarily follow. When it is a question of material goods, sincere love should, it is true, be disposed to share them even at considerable cost to self and one may soon suffer want of support. But however painful the results of his catering to the needs of the beloved, the lover suffers no mutilation or suppression of his fundamental will to advance the beloved. He cannot deny the act that is constitutive of his own being, i.e., willing himself for the sake of the other; and how could the effacement of the self automatically produce positive progress in the other? Recourse to voluntary self-limitation solves nothing.

All this brings us back to our original statement and calls

for this additional remark: the self is convinced that in love it can influence another center of consciousness and produce, to a degree, the growth of an interior character that exists for itself in his presence. Every lover has this ambition, and to take it away from him is to take away his love itself. Illusory or not, his intention rests on this fundamental belief in a transitive action of one consciousness on another.

A WILL TO MUTUAL PROMOTION

To love implies the desire to be loved, and in a certain sense, the fact of being loved. I am well aware that this double affirmation will cause some astonishment. Those who disagree with me will cry shame, as though I were introducing egoism into the heart of generosity. They will also accuse me of mistaking chimeras for realities; it is only too evident that affection is not always requited. However, I do not see how I can relinquish my paradoxes.

In my defense I will first expound and evaluate the contrary opinion. It has recently been brilliantly presented by Anders Nygren in *Agape and Eros.*[3] This Lutheran philosopher conceives of two kinds of love. One is *Eros,* the desire for the best: the aristocratic aspiration of the human self that would wish to raise itself to the level of the divine; it cannot be satisfied except by taking God Himself for its object. It is motivated by the perception of the beauty residing in this supreme object.

The other type of love is *Agape:* it is the gift and sacrifice of self for the loved one; it creates the value of its object; it is spontaneous and kind; it is not in the least motivated by the excellence of the beloved. Eros is centripetal; agape is centrifugal. They are two spiritual movements that have nothing in common.

This psychological opposition, continues the author, is rooted in history. The Greek philosophers knew eros; it was Christianity that revealed agape. Within the Greek perspective, love expresses man's nature and responds to his tendency toward perfection. We must not confuse the popular Venus with the celestial Venus: eros is, of course, noble. But it is a superior egoism, none the less. It postulates a human soul with a divine value buried in its depths; its goal is the divinization of the self. Through love, the soul is awakened to the desire to arrive at the absolute perfection from which it is exiled here below and for which it has an indestructible nostalgia. The lover is enamored of himself and therefore seeks to possess God in order to become divine. As for the love of other human beings, it can be, under these conditions, only an instrument for going toward self and toward God. The neighbor is a step on the ladder to the divine and we can appreciate our fellow men only insofar as they serve as means to our ascension: we love them *propter Deum*.

On the other hand, agape is the supernatural love emanating from God himself and subsisting in Him alone; it is bestowed on us gratuitously as a consequence of a sacrifice of the Most High. We who are the object of this love and receive it, are nothing but miserable creatures; our self has nothing lovable in itself, no rights, no intrinsic value. If we love our neighbor it is because the divine agape in us, by passing through us as an efficient and not as a final cause, impels us to act thus. In the true Christian tradition the other need not fear he will be treated as a simple means *propter Deum*. . . . Man is loved by man because the gift which comes from God demands it, and this gift is entirely disinterested: it is free of any egoistic infiltration. Agape alone respects and establishes true "philanthropy." This is strikingly evident in the evangelical precept to love one's enemies. Such an attitude is inconceivable to pagan philosophers, totally concerned as they are with allowing the delectable riches of the Good-in-itself to flow into them.

Nygren thinks that any synthesis of these two historic forms of love is impossible. St. Augustine forged a hybrid notion, *Caritas,* which mixes the Greek eros with the New Testament agape. Theologians of the Middle Ages often prolonged this error or erected it into a system; but the cement has never held. Their compromise raised insoluble difficulties and engendered repeated crises in the speculative order. However, these attempts have been useful, for their failure has helped place the exact notion of agape in bolder relief. Through successive "reforms" the Christian conscience has stood out with greater clarity, it has understood its own originality and supernatural character. The salvation of love is not from man, whose nature is all desire; salvation comes from heaven; it overcomes and transcends desire, for it is gift.

Such is Nygren's thesis: neat, elegant, and basically dualist. Here and there it lends itself to admirable developments. But I must admit that on the whole I cannot subscribe to it. My first objection is that it reduces man's role to nothing and makes impossible any dialogue between the creature and the Creator, or even between the beloved and the lover. It suppresses the very notion of a return of love. All it leaves is the divine solitude. Indeed, to what could our response to the Lord be reduced? An acceptance of grace? Submission? But is that love? If so it would be either eros or agape: if eros, the attitude of the beloved is egoistic and to be condemned. If agape, it ought to be in a form that can flow from the creature. Now, it seems to me that this is not a love that descends from God and has not yet met our being, but a love that is implanted in us to be reborn and rise again in newness toward God. Thus we are brought back either to the notion of a good eros excluded by Nygren or else to that kind of created grace that duplicates agape and makes us imitators of God by elevating our nature to a supernatural state without destroying its personal spontaneity. In its communion with God the self is saved from its supposed fundamental perversion; personality responds freely to Him who calls it; it is not a stranger to transcendence but blossoms forth in it. But at this point we do not understand in the same way as Nygren the vicissitudes of a divine love loving itself in us. So we abandon his thesis to save the possibility of a loving exchange.

There is a final hypothesis possible: that obedience to grace would be neither eros nor agape. But by definition it would no longer be love, since love, it is maintained, can take only these two forms. We must conclude, then, that for Nygren the creature loved by God is itself incapable of love. If God expects something from us it can be only the docility of the slave. Under these circumstances should the divine liberality be called a work of love? It is the omnipotence of an artist who brings passivities to light; it is not the gift of a goodness that causes personalities to unfold.

No doubt one could answer that the attitude of the soul

submissive to God has a name, and that that name is faith. However, the difficulty still remains. Either faith has, indeed, been aroused in us by divine charity without ever being called to consummation in an act of love (but this affirmation, hardening as it does the theological distinction between faith and charity, would have the paradoxical result of making Nygren more Catholic than the Catholics themselves: under pretext of respecting the originality of faith, the whole religious life of man would be impervious to love). Or else, on the contrary, in keeping with the tradition of the Reformation, faith is formed by charity, and that formula would have to be interpreted in this instance as the affirmation of a loving response by man to God (but then we find again in our supernatural state and, under cover of faith, the difficulties regarding eros and agape I have already pointed out). Thus we shall either have to reject the thesis or deny any particle of generosity in man.

Actually, dialogue is essential to the reciprocity of love, and if there is to be dialogue between the Creator and the creature, the creature must be something other than a necessary reflection or an automatic echo. He must be capable of disinterestedness, and that by free choice. This living response supposes that the loved one desires to share in the perfection of the supreme lover in order to offer him an autonomous image of it. In a word, the love of God urges us and compels us, not in order to constrain us as things, but to oblige us to be free.

Let us suppose that we have this liberty and that Nygren accepts it. His doctrine would not be any more satisfactory; it would lead straight to a new impasse and strip human beings of the dignity proper to them: the power to delight and to grieve their Creator. It makes any disappointment of the divine Lover impossible. If the gift alone counts, if true love is centrifugal, the attitude and response of the beloved matters little; the lover can only cease being interested in the use the beloved will make of his freedom.

By an odd coincidence we come upon that unforgettable passage in which Goethe exclaims: "If I love you, what is that to you?" No doubt this proud cry represents a lofty state of soul; between unilateral love and spiritual beggary Goethe chooses unilateral love, and rightly so. Reciprocity is elusive; he fails to achieve it and resigns himself to choose the lesser of two evils. This designates a makeshift and not the perfection of love. The inevitable consequence of his protestation is the challenge: "If you don't love me, what is that to me?"

All these haughty questions are dangerous. There are two ways of being disappointed: one is to feel oneself thwarted, the other is to discover the moral mediocrity of the one loved. Now these two ways merge into one for the perfectly loving soul; for, unresigned to evil, it says: "My satisfaction is your value; my sorrow is your refusal to fulfill the value that was in you and that my love wants to help you to realize to the fullest."

Finally, just as the gift of the Creator includes the desire to elevate the beloved toward the harmony He offers, so also the mounting desire that moves the beloved, leads him to seek supreme perfection and admit that it consists in generously giving oneself. There is an eros of the agape, a need to possess the spirit of dis-possession, a desire to find one's soul in losing it. Why should eros be only a will to monopolize and use? It is the desire of the best, and as such is destined not to use everything but to learn that it ought to serve the spirit of generosity. The contrast proposed by Nygren is a psychological error. He condemns eros, whereas it is only the limits imposed on eros that are condemnable, limits which a sincere eros itself condemns, since it discovers that its vocation is to be converted to generosity.

Setting aside these theological discussions, let us turn to the direct and more modest analysis of the reciprocity of centers of consciousness—it will lead to analogous conclusions. Above all, it leads us to believe that every lover wants to be loved and all love finds at least a minimum of reward.

1) There is a *minimum of reciprocity* in the fact that love originates in the perception of the lovableness of the beloved. If it is truly another that I love and not an impersonal quality pinned on him, it is he who, in a sense, has begun to love me. He has advanced me and enriched me simply by his very presence open to my perception. My love for him ought to begin in a kind of thanks, and I can tell him with the poet: *"C'est moi qui te dois tout, puisque c'est moi qui t'aime."* ("It is I who owe you everything since it is I who love you.")

It will be objected that this person does not even know that virtue has gone out of him, and he may be unaware of my existence. How can you say he is my benefactor? I answer: he has not willed me by name, he has not turned toward me as a result of a special decision, but he has given himself to the world, he has willed this in willing to display his activity and allow his personality to be glimpsed there. Thus it is that he has caused his being to shine in my own.

Nietzsche speaks of an enriching virtue—*schenkende Tugend*—emanating from certain personalities. This radiance is not the prerogative of a Socrates or a St. Francis of Assisi; it is inseparable from all personal existence. To be in the world is to be a minimum of goodness publicly exposed. Human centers of consciousness are hidden in many respects by the cosmic masquerade; but there is one aspect under which they cannot do otherwise than show themselves and communicate their share of excellence to those who contemplate them. There are so many tragic and absurd angles to the human condition that we can only rejoice to discover this happy feature of our destiny. To be in the world is *to be able* to dissimulate and to wreak havoc, that is true; but first of all, before ugliness sets in, it is to open one's soul to other souls and bring them an initial presence which is itself a gift. A countenance that appears is a reality surrendered, a secret cautiously unveiled, a value poured out and not taken back. Everyone knows there is a play of light behind the lattice wall, and in the weakest or most retiring mind there is a fundamental will that continues to sing the joy of this necessary and innocent gift. The person is an expression and a role: he soon learns to calculate his effects or to poison the atmosphere. But in the beginning he is unaware of his grimaces and is all freshness and trust. Love is always watching for this initial moment, and that is why it is born in mutuality even though it must often sink into solitude.

2) But love does not have a hermit's vocation; it always seeks a *maximum of reciprocity*.

The response that a person to whom I am attached can give me may exhibit four successive degrees:

At the lowest, the other responds to my will to promotion by the *simple fact of his existence and growth.* The little child or the unconscious patient may never be aware of the care I lavish on them. My reward is that they live; their very existence is a recompense.

Then there is the reciprocity that is already psychological if *the other is aware of my project,* even though he rejects it or, while being aware of it, does not know its author. I provide him with a new theme. I plant in his being a virtual personality. Whatever variations he may weave on the theme or whatever may be his ignorance of the fact that he received it from me, he has truly received it and the theme is truly in him. My loving intention remains in his presence, at least under the form of an anonymous ideal of his self. It is a path that may be barred or that he may choose not to take; but something of my will is, as it were, really knit into his substance. Newman wrote in this fashion on the subject of the kind of presence that faithful Christians can have even in their persecutors: "They have a friend of their own in each man's bosom, witnessing for them; even in those who treat them ill."[4] This statement is rich in meaning and expresses in a particular instance the larger truth I am trying to define.

3) At the third level of reciprocity the *thou ratifies the loving design of the I for the thou.* He has accepted the theme offered him, and the variations he composes are in harmony with it. It is thus that the disciple repays the master and the child honors the education he has received. It is not a question of copying an effect or slavishly aping a model but of adopting a spiritual orientation and freely responding to a source of inspiration.

4) Lastly, reciprocity is complete when *the beloved in turn wills the advancement of the lover* and turns back to him with the same intentness that had turned the lover toward him, choosing the lover's personal development as the goal of his activity. At this moment the circuit of love is complete.

If we now analyze the gift of self that characterized the impulse of the loving person, we see that that person implicitly wants the four degrees of reciprocity whose progression we have just noted. By the very fact that he wants to help another be himself, the lover seeks to obtain, insofar as circumstances and the attitude of the loved one permit, the perfect constitution of the full circuit of love. This is equivalent to saying that by loving he aims somehow to be loved: the two movements inevitably converge.

What does it mean to *give oneself to another?* It is to commit oneself to be concerned about him, to make him exist more fully. But the lover would deny the worth of his love did he not desire the beloved to share it and be loving in his turn. To will that the other be loving is to will that he love in me what makes me able and willing to love him; it is to will that he love me. "I belong to you" means: depend on me for yourself, I dedicate myself to you. But the expression is equivocal and it is logical that it be so. It also means: I depend on something in you to help me so that I can be worthy of you and useful to you. Help me to help you. I want you to be such that I, in my turn, can place myself in your hands and receive a greater value from you. By the fact that I attach myself to you, I make it possible for you to transform me for yourself. In one and the same act I believe in you and in myself; I hope in you and in myself; my love is an invocation that I address simultaneously to you and to me.

Doubtless, when I love you I first will that you be loveworthy and, perhaps, even that your generosity turn away from me, in order to turn toward the world and give it a greater value. It is thus in conjugal love and friendship: I want the other to be able to forget me temporarily, should that be necessary for him to better fulfill his duty; I wish, in certain circumstances, that he go to those who need him before he concerns himself with me who can do without his help; I wish, in a word, to be able to esteem him. This is particularly so in parental love: a popular saying has it that parents do not rear their children for themselves, and that love descends from the older to the younger generation instead of rising from the younger to the older. These aphorisms not only express a fact of nature, they indicate an order of duty. But by consenting to my request that he leave me, the beloved richly rewards me at the very moment he seems to ignore me. And at the end of his charitable action, will he not meet me again? As the object of his act will I ever be absent from his horizon? It is only from his work, and in appearance, that he had to exclude me. I am not excluded from the deeper impulse that inspired his work. It was from me he drew the noblest reason for his withdrawal, since it was I who said: "If you love me, leave me."

Neither sacrifices nor delays can shut me out from the circuit that would draw my beloved toward me—it would be contradictory if they could. The journey of the beloved will be complete only if it comes to an end in me after having encompassed, in a way, a universe of other selves.

Even in the cases in which a physical distance is morally indispensable to the work of love, the lover wishes implicitly that the beloved, while setting forth from him, should come back to him in the end. The four degrees of reciprocity indicated above are in the will of the lover from the beginning; but he cannot fully live them except by stages, and he would destroy the purity of his intention if he omitted the intermediate steps through pride or impatience.

Thus, in the gift of self the *I* enhances the *thou* and this constitutes an agape; and the *I* is enhanced by the *thou,* which constitutes an eros. This circle is inevitable. What is willed is a manner of being of the *thou* and the *I* which derives directly from the loving will and has its origin in it. A sincere eros leads to agape; a sincere agape brings us back to eros; each leads to the other while remaining present in the other, once it has led there. The lover who has understood the implications of eros does not desire the other as an instrument to be subordinated to his use, but as an end that is equal or perhaps superior to himself. An analogous statement is true for the lover inspired by agape. If we raise these statements to the level of the principle that sustains them, we discover their transcendent unity: Plotinus taught that God is eros itself; his definition, properly understood, is meant to be illuminated and completed by the Johannine word: "God is agape."

The love of self, therefore, is not necessarily a form of egoism. It should culminate in self-sacrifice and is indeed implied by it. The two ways, while apparently opposed to each other, are really complementary. In principle they are inseparable. But whence comes *the inveterate distrust of moralists with regard to one of these two?* These men are severe toward eros and well disposed toward agape. The reasons for their attitude are mysterious and more difficult to explain than one would think. The facts are clear and no educator can doubt them. To suggest to a child that he take as his ideal the fullest development of his personality is to risk making a hard-hearted person of him, unsympathetic and unfeeling. He may become an "angelic epicurean" but he will still be an egoist. On the other hand, to exhort him to self-sacrifice and renunciation is to point out a short cut to perfection and propose a healthier and safer method of education.

The facts are clear . . . it is the reason for them that is obscure, and we cannot be satisfied with an argument *in terrorem,* or a pious sermon by way of explanation. Why, then, is the cult of self so equivocal and so apt to turn us away from the fullness of love instead of leading us to it?

A first reply would be as follows: the love of self is a spontaneous, constant and incoercible tendency. The gift of self, on the other hand, is fragile; it demands effort, which alone is meritorious. —That reply is, basically, quite insufficient. Let us rid ourselves of our prejudices and look at things impartially. What do we observe? On the one hand, in order to reach its goal, the desire for the best demands a host of sacrifices and heroic decisions. The lower self must be constantly immolated to the higher. In Plato's temple of wisdom there is an altar for holocausts; and even Nietzsche, who downgrades the will-to-good in favor of the will-to-power, is not a gentle master in this respect: in order to fulfill himself he tears himself like a corybant. —On the other hand, is it true that self-sacrifice for the sake of others is a disposition that is parsimoniously distributed among mankind and always hard to cultivate? I would be tempted to believe the contrary. Altruistic tendencies are as spontaneous as the others. There is a prodigal sacrifice of self all around us. But how many of these sacrifices are blind or stupid! . . . Many people will deprive themselves of necessities and spend themselves recklessly for a dog or a parrot. There are some who, in times of disaster, would rather lose their lives than be separated from a favorite house plant. Agape, too, has its excesses, its mistakes in perspective, and its perversions, sometimes touching, sometimes scandalous. The solution must be sought elsewhere.

A second reply is more satisfactory. It would have us note the ease with which love, whether it be selfish desire or self-sacrifice, ceases to be directed toward a *thou* properly so-called, and turns to impersonal objects. Thus it is that we become attached to things or institutions without making of that attachment a means for advancing personal subjects but rather a frontier that limits and satisfies us. But if it is an impersonal being we love it is impossible to give it true autonomy. A plant, a dog, or even a social form, such as the fatherland or humanity, are not subjects endowed with a free inner life. They are not universal perspectives like you and me. It follows that the loved one is, in this case, unequal to the lover; and even if the lover were to immolate himself for an object of this kind, he would be using it much more than he would be serving it. The will to possess necessarily gets the better of the will to give. If I realize that my dog is a dog, I shall never be able to love him for himself as much as, or in the same way that, I love him for myself. A kind of generosity and even reciprocity may unite us, but they are not of the same species as when the *thou* is a person. There will be a difference of level between an eros that is personal and an agape that cannot be so. True, I can forget that my dog is a dog and naively treat him as a friend and equal. But this naivete is suspect: I pretend to be unaware that the dog is not a personal self because in that way I can imagine that I am dominating a free being. The love of animals, and of children, too, affords us, at little cost, what we obtain only with great difficulty in the love of adults: security.

Besides, this illusion will not restore the balance between the two aspects of love, self-centeredness and self-sacrifice, for the failure of a frank and total reciprocity between the loved one and myself maintains a difference of nature between my desire turned toward my subjectivity and my devotion turned toward the weak form of consciousness that is my dog's. Willy-nilly the reach of my devotion will be shortened and the level of my objective will be lowered; the love I have for myself will direct and utilize my devotion in a tyrannical fashion. And this is normal.

But the psychological habit we contract in our relations with natural creatures or social institutions is apt to contaminate our relations with personal beings. We are tempted to transpose into inter-human love a behavior that is unjustifiable, since it makes us regard the other as a thing or an idea, and leaves us on the periphery of his subjectivity. At last we understand why moralists distrust the ways of eros and warn against its dangers. We understand it all the better when we see how facts confirm their fears. The attitude proper to the pseudo-love that persons bear toward things often invades the mind and spoils the love one bears toward other persons.

This explanation is interesting; but it calls for additional comment. The great mystery is the malady that impels eros and agape to stop short in their elementary stages and lazily rest there. We lack ambition for ourselves and others. But to this weakness it shares with agape, eros adds another of its own. Love of self is more quickly and thoroughly corrupted than devotedness. Whenever there is gift there is inevitably self-desire, too: we love ourselves as being able to help the *thou* we have chosen. On the other hand, where there is love of self there is not necessarily gift also; I can love myself in such a manner as to rid myself of all devotedness to others. In this sense, any gift, mediocre though it be, involves a certain attention to the interests of the self, it considers them and respects them; while the love of self, if it is mediocre, can wrap itself up in a strictly private pleasure and preclude any turning toward others. It is greedy and in too great a hurry. Thus the spell of evil paralyzes eros more completely than it does agape.

Nevertheless, evil does profit from the growing pains that hamper agape. If I renounce the noble love of self, it is because of deep-seated inertia. If, on the contrary, I get discouraged in my generosity toward others, it is not only from a lack of energy that has its source in me (and for which I am to blame), it is also occasioned by the ingratitude I experience on the part of others or their refusal of the value I wish to offer them. The inclination to give oneself meets with obstacles from within and without; the love of self finds them only within; its value and success depend, ultimately, on the self alone. In both cases, the soul suffers defeat; but morality, which is concerned only with what depends on us, will insist on the duty to fight against egoism and profess an *a priori* mistrust of the search for self. Renunciation and devotedness will be, in its eyes, the sole way of access to virtue.

Abandoning these subtle, irritating discussions, we shall next consider the most frequent symptoms of the disease that strikes love. The first is bitter jealousy. The self strictly limits the scope of its generosity, it goes out to the *thou* to the exclusion of others or against them. The second symptom is a slowing down in the soul's ascent toward value, or a descent into the cheap marketable values of sensuality; it is a sealing off of approaches from above, a kind of monstrous insensibility to spiritual perfection. In jealousy and sloth are summed up the majority of love's tragedies. On the one hand there is belligerent tension and bitterness; on the other, the "vertiginous sweetness" of the rests or *decrescendos* that used to disturb Baudelaire.

To be cured, one has to go to the moralists. And the reform they propose will be first to stop loving one being at the expense of another. The avid and exclusive soul is already half converted when he can get along without rivals. Many couples feel the need of eliminating a third party and making him suffer in order to taste the happiness of their union. Their intimacy is heightened by these battles. This smiling sadism that persecutes everyone else in order to realize a sweeter life for two alone, has been little studied. It is, however, as mysterious as, and more frequent than, the frowning kind! Charles Lamb alludes to it humorously in his "A Bachelor's Complaint About the Behavior of Married

People": "What I am complaining about," he says, "is that you can't be in their company a moment without being made to feel, by some indirect hint or open avowal, that *you* are not the object of their preference."

Conversion is complete when it is realized that to truly love a person one must wish to make him infinitely lovable, for in this radical wish the need for all the values stands out. My partner will not be infinitely lovable unless he infinitely loves the universe of persons and makes himself worthy to be loved by them. I wish to raise him to a point where my jealousy is wiped out once and for all and where all the doors of the world are wide open to him. The will to advance the beloved is demanding: it tolerates neither pettiness nor laziness; it leads us much farther and higher than we had suspected at first; it implies, in effect, an unlimited development of the *I* and *thou;* and in the personal identity it pledges to confer on the lovers, it is the identity and development of all conscious beings that it is logically committed to promote, step by step, to the point where there is a mutual interpenetration of all by God and God by all.

LOVE LINKS PERSONS INTO A SPIRITUAL COMMUNITY

The reciprocity we have just analyzed is a journey of the *I* toward the *thou* and the *thou* toward the *I*. From the outset there is a vague perception of the bond that unites two centers of consciousness and all others in them. In a word, the relationship now takes the form of a *we*. But there are many forms of the *we*. F. Perroux distinguished the *we* of similitude (*I* as *thou*), the *we* of association (*I* with *thee*), the *we* of dilution (*I* in *thou*), and the *we* of love (*I* for *thee*). Though the list is incomplete and tentative,[5] it suffices to introduce the problem of the nature of the *we* of love and how it is distinguished from the others.

1) To understand its special character, let us take as an example an old man who loves the charm of a child. Shall we say that he seeks to acquire the child's charm and share it with him? Evidently not. It is not a question of fusing or confusing their respective domains. The old man wants the child to have its own charm and to keep it in the measure that it is a gift having its own nuances proper to the development of the little one. The child, who is attached to the old man, in his turn ratifies and advances, after a fashion, the wisdom or goodness of the old man. Each is happy to improve a wealth he does not possess in himself. Each has an asset in the other: it is a centrifugal possession. What is more, it is an existence of each self in the other, for it is their very being that grows and lives on in another being. Their inner will establishes itself in an outer world, and what is most intimate to it lodges in a stream of life different from their own. Thus it is in every personal love. It is hard for us to translate this situation into metaphorical language because it cannot be conceived as a community of bodily qualities or as a natural possession. We imagine presence in another as a good separate from the gift: thus we see the old man as possessing the loveliness of the child in the same way a wealthy man has his fortune at the bank. Matters of love are more subtle. The qualities which express each self do so only by being born in the other self and in developing for

his sake. It is through him that they come back to the lover in an atmosphere which is an offering in return.

The *we* of love is the very meeting of these two subjects whose having is in the other, and it is the awareness of this double, generous transposition that is its very being. More vital or more actual according to the degree of reciprocity attained, this is what characterizes all love. The communion of the subjects is but the coexistence of these two out-of-center series in which individual qualities can finally circulate in the continuity of persons. No other experience enables us to understand so clearly the reconciliation of the one and the many in the life of the spirit. *Aut duo, aut nemo.*

2) It follows that the *we* of love is a *heterogeneous* identity of the *I* and *thou*. It is the community of two subjects as subjects. Too often in the past philosophers have maintained that every identity is homogeneous. They regard as identical any two elements that we are unable to distinguish upon the most methodical examination. But while reason wishes to identify everything, reality opposes this reduction. The notion of an absolute identity may even be contradictory. This is what Plato was forced to conclude in his metaphysical dialogues on the same and the other. Closer to our own time, Bradley rejects identity as well as diversity in the world of appearances. And Meyerson admits that identity breaks down unless there is irrational diversity subsisting in contrast with it.

We should be spared many a philosophical dilemma if we admitted that identity is heterogeneous and does not concern objects but subjects. Just as Bergson abandoned the false continuity of homogeneity and introduced the idea of a profound continuity with irreducible aspects, it seems we must realize that true identity is heterogeneous and supposes the diversity of subjects and their irreplaceable character. Far from causing confusion, this identity, which is the identity of love, abolishes errors. It disengages and dissolves the inferior, woolly form of identity; it forces us to sacrifice what obstructs the originality of personal subjects and prevents them from being themselves. It does not rest on the similarity between its participants but on their harmonious originality. Certainly it leads us to state, without fear of presumption, that the *I is the thou,* but only in the perspective in which it *causes the thou to be,* and is itself willed by the *thou.* By this will, the subjects identify with each other, and do so only in the measure in which they become different.

3) On the other hand, the *we* of love is inactive in the sense that it does not create the *I* and *thou* but simply expresses their mutuality. Friendship is not something added to two friends like a third individual, or even like a third force separable from their two wills. It does not establish them in their love by a kind of feedback; it simply accompanies them; it is the spiritual nature of their persons.[6] We are tempted to believe the contrary because we thoughtlessly assimilate the community of minds with the community that results from a juridical contract sanctioning social engagements. It is quite true that the contract is separate from the contracting parties and subsequently binds them before the law no matter what changes may have occurred in their inner disposition. But though the loving exchange does constitute a new situation, it does not create it in the same way a contract would. It is in the very tissue of the subjects who make the agreement, and if they separate,

it is torn apart. It leaves them as the sparkling of the sea flees with the setting sun.

If the exchange is active, it is through the weight of the past that has been inscribed in a common biography and which, in this regard, is indestructible and active even in the separate biographies. The *we* is dynamic from another point of view: it is a broadened, stimulating awareness that urges its participants to further progress, with due regard for their free decision. It is not a prop that forces us to grow just so, nor a technique for retraining ourselves. It is an energy and an attraction inviting us to make a common effort toward the highest values. Its own impulse—if it can be said to have one of its own—is to perceive vaguely a superior power of identity, more cohesive than the one previously experienced. The *we* is more or less closely knit: each degree of union it expresses awakens the dread of disunion and impels us to seek an ever closer reciprocal belonging.

4) Finally, even though the subjective *we* may be indifferent, in principle, to the number of its associates and capable of an indefinite extension without its form undergoing any radical change, in the human condition the *we* seems to be limited to a dyad: subjective awareness does not achieve real reciprocity except between two personal beings. Such is our situation. The biblical notion of Adam and Eve is to be taken seriously. Even the dyad itself is weak, intermittent, and maintained in fragmentary fashion. *Nec sine te, nec tecum.* How often trajectories cross only to move apart from each other! Even the fairest climates have their fogs and tempests.

Naturally, there are many possible dyads (Eve and Abel, Abel and Cain, etc.). But the existence of a triad or a quadrad is rather problematical: I mean a community in which three or four individuals are simultaneously translucent to each other in such a way that each turns lovingly to the others as if they were but one and receives from them simultaneous and equal attention. The triad has the formula: a–b, a–c, b–c. The family group would seem to furnish its elementary type; but who will maintain that father, mother, and child are each able to think of the other two at the same time without some faltering on the part of one of the three? Two beings can unite personally in the devotion they have for a third person: the dyad accompanied by a "for him" is frequent. But does the third party then turn to the other two with the same refinement of perception and without any loss of contact?

This distribution, if it occurs at all, and if it truly concerns the will to mutual advancement, is certainly very unstable. Either there is a swift passage from one dyad to another, or the triad descends below the personal level we are presently considering and sinks into a confused impression of community, as in a team or a group. In that case it is the idea of a common task and not their individual selves that unites the members of the group. In place of the subjective *we* there is substituted, in a sense, the image of the other or others, i.e., an objective *us*. It is by the mediation of an objective *us* and the shift from one dyad to another that love maintains its power to unite morally all men, in spite of their discontinuity, and according to the demands already implicit in the sincere relationship between two lovers. But these vast horizons are always enclosed in a more humble form; they are reflected obliquely in the narrow mirror of the dyad.

NOTES

1. We should remember that for Scheler the person is ruthlessly separated from psychic self-awareness. It is a supra-conscious center of heterogeneous intentional acts (for example, sentiments and representations). It follows that certain social realities—nations for instance—can be persons. I would have numerous reserves to make about this divorce and this corollary. Of course the person does not seem to me to be identical with what is ordinarily called psychic awareness, but it does involve a certain kind of awareness: the kind inherent in an I and diffusing the I in the psychic life under the form of the *self*. But it is only in metaphor that one can speak of a subjectivity of this kind with reference to social groups.

2. I have made use of Scheler's most important work on the subject, *Nature et formes de la sympathie* (Paris, 1928). However he seems to have broadened his views in certain respects when, in other works, he opposes the creative love of Christians to the preservative love of the Greeks. See *Le Sens de la souffrance* (Paris, 1936), pp. 154–5 and *passim*. (Translator's note: *Nature et formes de la sympathie* is available in English translation under the title *The Nature of Sympathy*, translated from the original German by Peter Heath (New Haven, Yale U. Press, 1954).

3. Trans. Philip S. Watson (2 vols., Philadelphia, Westminster, 1953).

4. John Henry Newman, *Selection. Parochial and Plain Sermons* (London, 1900), p. 404.

5. F. Perroux and R. Prieur, *Communauté et société* (Paris, 1941), p. 12. See ch. 7, for an attempt at a more detailed classification of the varieties of collective consciousness.

6. All proportion guarded, the *we* is here an image of what theologians call the nature of God in the Trinity.

2 ✧ *The Work of Love*

If we could overlook the limitations of earthly existence, we might apply the preceding considerations to pure spirits. We have tried to highlight the spiritual essence of the love relationship. However, human love is incarnate; it is not fulfilled in a misty Eden but in a material and violent world. It seeks and finds its identity by representing itself to itself in another nature. The values it pursues come to it through a mass of physical and social conditions that alternately conceal and reveal it. It is subject to ambiguity. Our bio-social existence menaces and sweeps personal love into its vortex and stifles it there. But the menace can be transformed into an ally if we choose. The whole material order can collaborate in achieving the noblest goal of conscious beings, and this collaboration is both necessary and dangerous. It is this alliance that accounts for the gravity of human option and enables us to create ourselves by our free acts.

We may express the same truth in another way by saying that our loves are inscribed in a task. A glance or a polite gesture is already a kind of work whereby the interior at-

37

titude is objectified. This is even more true in the offering of gifts, the sharing of goods, and the heroic sacrifice of sensible or spiritual goods for the loved one. The same internal logic impels conscious beings to express their mutuality by a project that goes beyond their immediate concerns: for example, the rearing of a family, or the joint dedication to a common social or religious cause.

When sex life intervenes in the love of persons it is only as an intermediary work in which love is fulfilled. It brings nothing essentially new to the situation of concrete love which must always be incarnate in nature. But sexuality is a particularly vigorous and demanding association. There, certainly, love will have two poles: the one cordial and the other carnal. It must succeed in the difficult enterprise of making the first dominate the second, and spiritualizing the second even while it incarnates the first. Constantly in danger of being engulfed in this instinctual exchange, love can, on the other hand, find in it an extraordinary stimulus that no other incarnation (in the work of friendship or benevolence, for example) could give it.[1]

THE WORK OF LOVE CONSIDERED FROM THE VIEWPOINT OF THE LOVING SELF

The lover can carry out his will to advance the other only through intermediaries, for he is separated from the *thou* by nature. To overcome nature's opacity, hostile to his purpose, he must create a work. And this for two reasons: first, to express his love and make it perceptible to the beloved; second, to advance the interests of the beloved and provide him or her with the instruments of his or her own development. In these two cases the loving self uses things for the sake of persons and introduces into his act an uncertain form of causality. Instead of acting directly on another consciousness he operates on and through natural forces. He produces or destroys sensible forms to suggest his intention and induce his project in the other. In short, he becomes an artificer. The very language by which one declares one's love is work of this kind, the most subtle of the creations of *homo faber*.

But there is no intrinsic proportion between these utterances and the disposition of minds: the realm of motion is not the realm of thought; if the first is placed at the service of the second, the resulting correspondence is merely empirical; if it offers certain constant aspects, it is the role of induction to discover them in the sequence of events. A totally spiritual influence between persons would imply, on the contrary, a simple form of causality, a pure communion without communication of an intermediary kind.

In this pure communion of centers of consciousness, the act of the *I* would immediately alter the situation of the *thou*, without allowing the slightest deformation of the causal intention. When the influence is directly spiritual, a single cause can produce only a single effect. The intention of the *I* flies toward the *thou* like an arrow to strike at his heart. It is like those happy moments of artistic inspiration in which a writer creates a character without any hesitation and with a single stroke presents an unforgettable personality perfectly fulfilling the author's esthetic desire. His artifact is a faithful reflection of his mental image.

In incarnated influence, action does not have this nice certainty; its result is problematic. An intention may never attain the fullness of its effect. This is the case of unhappy or ineffectual love; the cause never succeeds in going out of itself. Or again, a single cause may produce a number of unforeseen and different effects; in love's qui-pro-quos a helpful gesture may be wrongly interpreted, a generous act may result in misfortune for the beloved. . . . Finally, the same effect may result from different causes: lies or hatred, for example, may scatter blessings in some instances (though beneficence normally flows from benevolence, that is, from what is opposed to lying and hate). From the moral standpoint, a child profits from the goodness shown him, but occasionally, by a strange paradox, from bad example, too.

The mind soon discerns this irrational diversity. Whether it be to express his love or be of use to his beloved, man must master the techniques of nature and use them as best he can for his spiritual purposes. Thus he will necessarily resort to an interplay of *favors* and *sacrifice.* But these means are also temptations; these values can be changed into forces of devaluation. Hence the person is perpetually attracted to a mode of action in which his initial impulse is to buckle or warp.

Instead of using the gift to reveal himself in his true light, he may use it to create a false light or invent an alibi. Instead of helping, he deceives the loved one. Let us examine some of these dangers.

The most common danger lies in a technique of seduction, i.e., of flattery or coquetry. This is encountered not only in relations between the sexes but in interpersonal relations of any kind. Is not love vitiated at every turn by tyranny and servitude? It seems doomed to give birth to situations contrary to its essence and to forge chains that must be broken by constant reform. The lover is an admirer; he quickly reaches the point where he will deceive the other by exaggerating the other's lovable qualities: this is *flattery,* the most seductive of errors and the ordinary starting point in the pathology of the emotions. Then, to this primary aspect of courtesy is added a secondary one: the lover tries to deceive himself about the qualities and intentions of the beloved. This is *loving illusion,* the most touching of errors.

Coquetry enters from the opposite side. Its principal form consists in deceiving the other about one's own intentions and worth; in order to be loved, the lover will try to dazzle the other; he will indulge in bragging—one of the most odious deviations of the heart. Finally, the secondary aspect of coquetry will give us illusions about ourselves and expose us to the phantoms of personal vanity, the most stupid of faults.

If the maneuvers succeed, a false reciprocity will ensue. The beloved will be asked to accept gifts without loving the giver. This procedure may be reinforced by mutual blackmail in which the stake is not the communion of the subjects but the exchange and delivery of a camouflaged image which they offer each other, or pretend to give to themselves, as if they had been able to siphon off their pure subjectivity. They will alternately offer and demand presents which will be the specious symbols of each self. Two simulated sacrifices will mimic in mutual hypocrisy what should be the transparent simplicity of perfect gifts. Subsequently, in the course of this ingenious game, the partners will enter into a tacit complicity, each accepting to be both deceiver and deceived. Both will agree to behave as if the sentiments they exchange were of the first quality; this is the ignominious intoxication by which a couple agrees to keep up a mutual lie. They want desperately to succeed, and when they cannot, they make a pretense at success.

In a defense at once superficial and cynical, Erasmus delights in all this misery: "What is it when one kisses the wart on his mistress' nose? When a father shall swear his squint-eyed child is more lovely than Venus? What is this, I say, but mere folly? And so, perhaps you'll cry, it is; and yet 'tis this only that joins friends together and continues them so joined. . . . What divorces, or what not worse than that, would daily happen were not the converse between a man and his wife supported and cherished by flattery, jesting, dissimulating, and such like playing the fool?"[2]

In reality, the compromises of everyday life are a smile superimposed on a secret anguish. Their tragi-comic nature is not a simple contamination of interpersonal ends by interpersonal means, nor a pretense without sense or seriousness. It is really much more, since it is a spiritual fraud. Materialism in love has no other cause, and its consequence is to close the mind to the attainment of the highest values. The perversion is all the more deadly because this halt in the upward climb may well be accompanied by a readiness to dialogue in depth. A false communion of souls has its vicissitudes and revelations. It lays open the field of the psyche and plows it in every direction; it produces an astonishing fertility that is very gratifying to amateur psychologists.

It is easy to imitate Erasmus and ridicule the lovers. Usually it would be more just to excuse and pity them. Sincere love is often unnoticed or disdained; a vast amount of unexpended generosity then accumulates and with it the temptation to compensate for the underestimation of others by an overestimation of self by self. There is an attempt to remedy the wrong suffered by a wrong committed. The ruse to outbid the other enters the fruit like a worm.

Perversion comes about all the more easily because in its origins it is almost identical with a normal disposition. In fact, one becomes a sincere benefactor only by forcing oneself, as it were, to create benefits. The lover does not say, "I love you," just because he already loves, but in order to love better. And even if he gave the whole world to his beloved, his token would still involve more of hope than of reality. For love is developed by the works that it *will* do and that go beyond the initial stage. Its substance lies always ahead in the infinite project it undertakes; it is never completed; its manifestations are at once a recapitulation of the past, and the seed of the future. No word, no act, can contain all they promise. Henceforth, it is difficult to draw the line between good and bad faith. Fiction is inevitable in the evolution of a loving consciousness and can even help it. But how easy it is to becloud a "pure" fiction! From the moment one rests in it, it is no longer a docile means but an insidious falsehood.

Thus, simple and honest souls are often bewildered in the presence of their first love: the reason the young girl hesitates at the moment she utters her first *yes* is often that she fears to lie by saying more than she has actually felt. Poised at the edge of the unknown, she must enter it as if it had already been explored; she must swear to the existence of what she does not yet know and may never know. Sensitive natures are at first tempted to disclaim competence in the matter; they need courage to overcome this scruple. But only foolish natures imagine that all that is needed is an instantaneous infatuation, considering this the essential of love. Only false natures take pleasure in infatuation and exploit the intoxication of the passion of the moment, as if infinite love could descend whole and entire in the present and do without the work of the future to arrive at its fullness in the human soul.

All the weaknesses we have examined thus far are simply exaggerations of normal reactions. But there is another series of errors indicating a more radical perversion of the work of love: the errors of those who, in order to obtain the gift of the beloved, employ the techniques of suffering for selfish purposes: the lover will torture the loved one or else turn his blows against himself and expect from this physical and mental cruelty an even greater pleasure. Often allied to the quest of sexual pleasure, these modes of action have, nevertheless, a wider application to the psychology of love in general. Is it not disturbing, for example, that in order to consolidate one's bent and give it consistence, nothing works so well as the barb of a cruel anxiety? Passion delights in living, or in making the other live, in perpetual fear, stirring up torments of doubt in the other, or nursing them in oneself. Anxiety crystallizes affection.

Jean-Paul Sartre has devoted a number of provocative pages to the analysis of sadism and masochism. He sees in them two ineffectual processes for escaping a contradiction having its source in love itself. The sadist discovers his inability to act on the freedom of the other while that other, his victim, watches him; he fails, furthermore, because he wants to do the impossible and make all the subjectivity of his partner pass into her body; he would transform the flesh of the other into an instrument in order to seize her living body-ness, which however can never be a tool. The efforts of the masochist are no more successful. He tries to persuade himself that he has been reduced to the state of object for the other; he attempts to abdicate his own transcendence, but never succeeds: his active freedom leads to the denial that he makes of his liberty and commands the strategy of his acts; he no longer aims at acting on others insofar as the others regard themselves as objects relative to him; but in order to convince the others and make them his accomplices he treats them as objects and ceases to be passive; finally, he is overwhelmed to the point of anguish by his own inalienable subjectivity.

These vices are failures, and the pleasure of vice is the pleasure of failure. Perhaps we can follow Sartre up to this point. But drawn by metaphysical principles quite different from the ones that guided our preceding study, he makes vice the consequence of a serious flaw presumed to be in love itself. Let us consider his thesis for a moment. I do not think it a distortion of his main idea to say that for him love is an absurdity that drags us back to solitude. It is an absurdity: for we struggle to be loved freely, a thing which is contradictory, or at least illusory. It leads us to solitude; for to love is to wish to be loved, and to wish to be loved is to bend the other to our own will; thus we end where we had begun.

Let us now explain this governing principle. Love is an imperialism of the person who is dedicated to the impossible task of reconciling constraint and liberty, i.e., of acting on the liberty of the other. It "does not demand the abolition of the other's freedom, but rather his enslavement as freedom; that is, freedom's self-enslavement."[3] The other holds the secret of what I am, in this sense, that I know myself to be *observed* by him; this self, which is my being-for-others, is what I should like to possess; to do this I seek to absorb the freedom of the other who holds my secret. But how can one possess a freedom as such? I would simultaneously have to be the cause of the *thou* and refuse to be its cause. Since this is impossible I look for compromises but find none that satisfies. The lover would like to be only the occasional cause of the other's gift, while conferring on himself all the values of the world in the eyes of the other. In short, he has to become a seducer, seeing love only as seduction, that is, the will to be loved. He is guided by an unrealizable ideal: in essence he is mixed up in the fraud, "since to love is to will to be loved, hence to wish that the other wish that I love him" (p. 377). The lover is cast back on his own will; he returns to enclose himself in his own subjective and solitary project; he does not transcend the transcendence of the other any more than he suppresses his own transcendence in the eyes of the other. This alone would justify our speaking of a failure of love, without even invoking the ever possible reawakening of the beloved and the insecurity that results for the couple from the interventions of outsiders or the force of circumstances.

It is not hard to understand that love thus conceived is permeated with pain. Suffering is for lovers a means of desperately strengthening the illusion that their very venture is matter for sacrificial offering. In his day, Maurras maintained in one of his *Contes Philosophiques* ("Myrto") that love, under any form, is impossible, whether it be popular, Platonic, or Christian. For Maurras, the tortures that result from love are in a large measure the vengeance the natural order wreaks on the folly of our hoping to unite two individual efforts in an absolute and reciprocal commitment. We suffer this vengeance in a thousand painful ricochets. According to Sartre, we not only endure this vengeance, we actually call torture to our rescue and use it as a kind of magic that ultimately proves to be vain and ineffectual. But do the points these two authors make authorize their sweeping conclusions? They simply show that the work through which love is expressed is always inadequate to love's essence, and that to stop at the work would be to annihilate love. Possession is centripetal with these authors; it does not have the centrifugal character we have noted in every truly loving reciprocity, at least in its conscious purpose, if not in the means it must employ to express and perfect itself. It is quite true that outward manifestation must alienate love temporarily and give it an appearance of a natural mastery and slavery; but if this were not the case, the means would be confused with the end and love would not be incarnate in a world that can only deny it at the outset. But what is for us a means involving a temptation, is for Sartre an end revealing an incompatibility. As I see it, suffering intervenes of necessity, only to warn the loving persons of the deficiency of their work; as he sees it, suffering is the presence of a battle to the death, the bitterness behind the challenge. In the depths of the infinite that it invites us to penetrate, there is for him only a promise of deception and nothingness; for me, there is the pledge of perfection and fulfillment.

Furthermore, Sartre seems to avoid the study of satisfied reciprocity. He gives it only a half page and explains it incidentally, merely in passing. I am not speaking of an attempt at reciprocity which, according to him, is certainly inherent in the attempt to love, but of the twofold reciprocity of happy lovers. This joy, "if it exists," Sartre says, results when the other *also* decides to love me; henceforth we agree on a double challenge, but we find ourselves by that very fact on the fragile bridge of a common joy: the joy of feeling ourselves loved, i.e., of feeling justified in our existence, because we regard our whole being as a good that we generously offer to the desire of the other. "I am because I give myself away. These beloved veins on my hands exist beneficently. How good I am to have eyes, hair, eyebrows and to lavish them away tirelessly in an overflow of generosity, to the tireless desire which the Other freely makes himself to be" (p. 371).

These lines are as fierce as those of a Father of the Church hard on the trail of our concupiscences. But beneath this caricature do we not discern an avowal? There really are, then, fleeting glimpses of joy and partial successes? There is, then, an occasional union of two successes? It is illuminating that this phenomenon occurs in the experience of giving. I know very well that in this general dialectic the sharing of the gift is an unstable phase or, in any case, a secondary aspect dominated by the power of seduction. Still, in presence of the gift, the author's pessimism must disappear. The loving ideal has become a reality, and love is no longer a square circle.

But Sartre has decided to define love by possession rather than promotion. These two terms are not given equal importance in his doctrine. That is why I wonder whether, despite appearances, his doctrine treats of love or substitutes for love. Some critics detect the odor of sulphur in his writings; for my part I find them terribly leaden, with an annoying tendency to tarnish or dull the few golden rays of existence. To decide this issue one would have to judge his whole metaphysics of consciousness—to which I, for my part, would oppose another metaphysics. He is too good a philosopher to forget a single element in the study of a question. Many of his texts, consequently, strike me as being true. But their context is not the same as mine, and I take exception to the over-all meaning. Beginning with the "look" as a fundamental form of concrete relationships with others, he classifies all intersubjectivity *a priori* as a threat; and he decides beforehand that any real continuity between persons is impossible. But the experience of love as a will to promote the freedom of the other is, on the contrary, proof to me of this continuity, at least in principle. If it is true that the freedom of the beloved is developed in the efficacious will of the lover, it reconciles constraint with liberty in the mystery of influence. Instead of establishing the problem in the conflict of minds I am inclined to suppress the exaggerated distance Sartre places between the objective *thee* and subjective *thou,* the objective *me* and subjective *I,* and to strengthen, on the contrary, the passage he builds between *being-for-other* and *being-for-self* in a sense that is really not strictly his. Finally, noting as he does, that the will to love implies the will to be loved, I no longer have to conclude that the subjects are in a radical solitude, since this solitude is inevitably peopled the moment it takes on value. Freedom cannot fully will itself without willing other freedoms. Can it even conceive itself other than as originating as the effect of a generous Will, and not as an unredeemed, culpable "protuberance" rooted bizarrely in the world, only to negate it and perish with it?

Without pretending to answer this last question and

justify my answer here and now, I will at least point out that my difference of position does not prevent my assigning to suffering a role in the work of love. I even assign it two roles, since it is allied to the exercise of generosity as well as to the failure of tyranny. Generosity not only suffers from the mediocrity of the other, it also groans under the lover's inability to be infinitely generous. One must submit to being bruised by the exterior obstacles that hinder the full development of the beloved; one must above all undergo the deep surgery of misunderstanding and cowardice in the other and in oneself. How often, for a thousand different reasons, does love not feel, in the words of Alfred de Vigny, *"taciturne et toujours menacé"*? How often it verges on despair and trembles before a corpse—or, what is worse, before a betrayal!

Every man must know an hour of darkness in which, blinded by the world's often systematic deceit, he is tempted to cry out: "I shall never have but one spouse, death; our betrothal will last as long as I live and our marriage will be eternal." But the shadows do not completely obscure the light of life, and the temptation of nihilism is no proof that nothing exists. The sorrow that penetrates the noblest of our sentiments and reveals its infinite depth never *defines* it except in appearance: one might just as well insist that the thorns are the rose. To make unhappiness the essence, or even the essential consequence, of our spontaneous movement toward the other is, as I see it, mere sophistry. No matter how distressing the tears, no matter how copiously and long they flow, they are born of a paradoxical hope whose sweetness is inexplorable yet invincible. To absorb so many sorrows we must go beyond them; exile is bitter only if there is a paradise. The truth is that the invisible soul of the mutual will to promote the other can never be completely identified with the painful task in which it is incarnate and which is always constricted, multiple, and untractable at one point or another. It is all the more true that the systematic exploitations of suffering in the form of sadism or masochism are not corollaries but perils of the disposition to love. It is owing to the conditions of love's task that the spirit can be involved in it; it is in order to fulfill its own generous and heroic vocation that the spirit must also free itself from it.

Another danger would be to try to precipitate success in love by a will to moral devaluation. Not only can the *I* will the abasement of the *thou* the better to preserve and enjoy their pact; he may make himself ignoble in order to facilitate the triumph of the *thou*. I should like to pause to study the latter case, because it is the least common and the most tragic. In a classic poem the English poet Richard Lovelace, says:

> *I could not love thee, dear, so much*
> *Loved I not honour more.*

According to the context, the idea of Lovelace is, perhaps, not that he loves honor more than his mistress, but that his love for her is the motive that intensifies his sense of duty, whether his mistress likes it or not.[4] Now, it happens that the lover reverses the idea expressed by Lovelace and extracts from his love the reason for his abasement. Sometimes, under a facile and, happily, purely verbal form, lovers may declare themselves ready to commit any misdeeds or crimes to prove to each other the sincerity of their attachment. But in real life these protestations may be actually carried out. . . . It may even happen that their fulfillment has a certain grandeur. . . . There are crimes of love that have a disturbing and undeniable nobility: such, for example, as engaging in dishonest transactions to afford more comforts for one's spouse or a better education for the children. Such dishonorable action may often flow from vulgar complacency or stupid vanity. But this is not always the case; crime may bear the imprint of a terrible generosity that impels a lover to become immoral himself in order to free a cherished but weak friend from immoral surroundings: he is ready to sacrifice his own honor to purchase the good of the loved one, even at the expense of losing face before God, men, and the beloved. Just as he would wish to exhaust his physical strength, so he considers himself authorized to commit any fault and even moral suicide to assure not only the physical well-being of a friend, but also his or her potentiality for spiritual growth.

At the heroic summit of this extravagant generosity, we are at first tempted to place St. Paul's desire "to be anathema for his brethren." Is this not the most prodigious flight of pure love? Mystics have often taken this prayer seriously and the Middle Ages abound in discussions on it. We may believe that for St. Paul and the more lucid among his disciples the offering thus formulated was subordinated to the good pleasure of God. Divine perfection cannot grant such prayers according to the letter, but only the spirit. Several saints have prayed thus and no doubt did so sincerely, in a kind of spiritual agony, from the depths of their heart and not from the tips of their lips. But they were expressing thereby their profound awareness of being unable to achieve a maximal reciprocity except by the cruelest stripping of self; they wished to be cut off from God Himself for the sake of the sinner; that is, to accept the trial of a perpetual night so that the sinner might see the light. The God they banish from their consolations, they find again in the depths of their act which is the very spirit of the most active charity. It is only an unreal separation from God and the sinner; they desire exile and abasement only as a passionate means of purifying themselves, and in that greater purity God immediately appears. The sinner himself, mysteriously touched by this conversion of the saint, cannot help being drawn closer to the one who had made himself anathema for his sake.

There is an absolute difference between the will to be anathema and what we call a crime of love. If we consider only the frequent case of conscience in which a father does not hesitate to amass wealth dishonestly so as to better house and clothe his children, we suspect that honor is destroyed in every part if it is set aside in any part. Good must be at the root of the father's industrial or commercial enterprise if it is to be at the root of his fatherly devotion. Base means are in reality rival ends; and when one thinks he is choosing means to an end he is substituting another end for the first one. The lover who dishonors himself in the marketplace contradicts himself in the home: he is a scandal to the loved one; and even if the loved one knew nothing of it, or approved it, a will that would advance another at this price is divided and does not give itself totally. Certainly, it is impossible here below to escape tragic dilemmas in which generous principles do not suffice to enlighten us. Moralists are quick to suppress uncertainty with a stroke of the pen, as if there were recipes for seeing clearly in cases of conscience. In the last analysis a man is always alone when it is a question of resolving his concrete difficulties. . . . But the art of sound conduct is precisely to overcome the initial obstacles of the loving task and go beyond its abstract elements. Moral abdication of the self to the other is a simplistic refusal to resolve problems according to the total spirit of love; it is a retreat that leaves us facing a difficulty without trying to transform any of its elements. It is by a quite different attitude that kind acts and sacrifice reach their moral goal.

THE WORK OF LOVE FROM THE VIEWPOINT OF THE WE

When lovers have reached a sufficient degree of reciprocity they can make explicit agreements and enter on a common enterprise. What ends will their efforts serve?

First of all, it will have as its object to *consolidate* the mutuality already achieved. Such, in part, is the function of vows, contracts, and juridical institutions in general, when they have a psychological aspect. Symbols, like the celebration of anniversaries and the exchange of rings in marriage, serve the same end. Thanks to these aids the union is protected against the intermittences of the heart and is less likely to be dissolved or revert to indifference. Safeguards of this kind resemble the net spread to catch the acrobat in case he falls; but it is a net of sacred memories, or at least a means of stirring the memory by a physical presence and conferring on the majesty of past promises the immutable character of things.

Symbols also set a value on future commitments and lead

the couple to pledge themselves to undertake together a task that goes beyond the immediate interest of either party. The birth and education of children is the simplest example of this widening of love's horizon. The dyad works for a third party, and calls new dyads into being. Or again, it devotes itself to a social cause of its own choice, be it professional or civic; this it does in a context not always of its own choosing but to which it must agree at the time.

Love's work has a number of elements and conditions. It also has its risks. The limits within which one works may be too constricting and, instead of being a means to life, may become an unbearable yoke substituting empty obligation for the fullness of love. Again, the creative aspect of the project may not fit the framework, and thus lack the support needed for its completion. It would be easy to give illustrations of these virtual oppositions: Claudel, for example, shows it forcefully in *Le Partage de Midi*,[5] where he so radically distinguishes between marriage and sex love. In a different context, one could show the difference between the initial phase of a community (the beginnings of a religious order, for instance) when creative activity dominates, and the later phases, when regulations take precedence over plasticity.

The repetition and sameness characteristic of a shared task oblige the collaborators to compensate their automatisms by a desire for reform and progress. They must maintain the structure at the service of the spirit and make it not only a repository for past aspirations but also a cradle for future dynamic activity. Suppleness and fidelity are equally indispensable in love's life and work.

At the point we are considering, the work is always associated with a social order and modifies it in a personal way. Step by step, our study leads us to a definition of civilization. The civilizing movement consists in creating a new cycle of personal determinations and inserting it in the preceding cycle: civilization is but the impregnation of the conditions of collective life by successive personal deposits. The antecedent cycle of these conditions constitutes natural society for the persons living in it; and the subsequent cycle constitutes personal society insofar as it can be expressed and fixed in objective institutions.

The intervention of the personal order in the cycles of natural society profoundly modifies the form of human progress. The latter, when considered in the vital spontaneity of evolution, proceeds by way of rise and decline. But civilization, which derives from an intelligent action, is at once more precarious, because it is no longer a blind force, and more capable of indefinite development, because the spirit aims directly at an eternal goal. To the cyclic progress of life is substituted the *possibility* of a continuous improvement inherent in human civilization and manifesting the superiority of the rational community over the instinctive one. On the one hand there is the seasonal rhythm of periodic returns; on the other, a fragile but free accumulation of beneficial effects on a straight and limitless line.

The person is always above and beyond natural society; he never has that society for his end. But he uses civilization as a means to the unfolding of new personal values in which his communitarian acts are expressed. When the work of the self in society yields to the living work of a *we,* what has just been said about the eminent value of persons is all the more true: love, at the very outset, gives to society more than it receives from it and attempts to penetrate it for the benefit of persons. This is where Hegel's philosophy, which subordinates persons to the nation or state, contradicts the order of values implied in a philosophy of personal love, although Hegel has done so much, in other ways, to justify the idea of an infinite personality.

An important corollary of this thesis concerns the notion of justice and its relation to charity. If charity creates social sedimentations, there is a whole aspect of civilization by which society is the history of charity. And justice then represents the present level of work accomplished by charity in civilization. It has a static aspect, since it is a matter of record; but it is also an historical effect and retains the residual impulse of the charitable act of which it is the trajectory. This impulse is manifested in the resistance of civilization to any descent on the ladder of historical achievements. Hence, justice is a kind of charity maintaining its conquests without going beyond them. It stops at the present and is blind to the future, or else it only conserves the present according to past principles that expand like coil springs and reveal all their analytic consequences. Justice is a blindfolded charity, a stubbornly active memory that creates nothing, but settles old accounts with severe precision. The moralist observes this pressure of justice in law, and when he considers it in consciousness, where it is a virtue, he can define it as a resistance to retreat on the road already traveled by the ancestral work of love.

Too often the static aspect of justice makes us forget its origin and nature. In the present of the established fact man thinks he discovers the lineaments of an eternal content, as if all the determinations of human nature had already been fully revealed. In reality, what is fixed in the content of justice is the part of our nature that the articulate past of personal love has affirmed most obstinately. Justice itself, if it is separated from time, cannot be studied without falling into mere verbiage, for it is an incessant transition of the instinctive society that precedes the person, to the action of the persons who civilize society by love. Just aspiration is *a priori,* but just determination is a contingent product. The ideal of justice, its eternal and non-temporary *a priori,* would be to get rid of all the patterns imposed on the loving work by nature and become itself the immaculate body of love in the kingdom of persons. This conquest of the external world by justice would not obliterate the historic character of the content of justice; it would finally bring it to light.

NOTES

1. The division of the sexes, remarks Soloviev, is not universal in nature; it is accomplished by a love that has as its purpose, in the human order at least, "the justification and deliverance of individuality by the sacrifice of egoism" (*The Meaning of Love,* trans., J. Marshall [London, 1945], p. 22). The idea is profound, but the proper end of conjugal union is above all the continuation of the species; the other ends of marriage cannot be radically detached from it.

2. Desiderius Erasmus, *The Praise of Folly,* trans. John Wilson (Ann Arbor, U. of Michigan, 1958), pp. 30, 32.

3. J. P. Sartre, *L'Etre et le néant* (Paris: Gallimard, 1943); English translation by Hazel E. Barnes, *Being and Nothingness* (New York, Philosophical Library, 1956), p. 403.

4. Cf. J. E. McTaggart, *Philosophical Studies* (New York, Longmans 1934), p. 256.

5. English title: *Break of Noon;* in Paul Claudel, *Two Dramas: Break of Noon, The Tidings Brought to Mary,* trans. Wallace Fowlie (Chicago, Regnery, 1960).

3 ⋄ *The Value of Love*

We have already noted that love pursues a value or reposes in it when it has found it. Precisely what value does it seek? This is the first question we must take up. In the second place, what value does this pursuit or satisfaction possess? That is to say, what value does love itself have? This second question reveals a final one: what reality does the value of love actually have?

WHAT DOES LOVE SEEK?

The inner logic of love impels it to develop until it has achieved the total fulfillment of its potentialities. It is not inevitable that it reach its utmost limits, for every human being is free up to a certain point to oppose it or respect it or, more exactly, to sink or rise in the current of love that bears him along. But each time we correspond to the essential demands of that impulse we are aware of implicitly willing the infinite perfection of the beloved and, indirectly, of ourself as loving. We commit ourself to make the other

59

and ourself utterly lovable and loving. But for a consciousness to be so it must embrace the whole universe and strive for the promotion of all other centers of consciousness according to the same value system. The human love of one person leads to the love of all persons. First of all, it wishes their existence and makes it an initial value. Next, it desires that their perfection or eternal essence be revealed, for it is through this eternal essence that the successive images of the ideal it has of itself are manifested to the discriminating conscience. Finally, love desires the autonomous development of individuals in time to be in as harmonious accord as possible with that ideal, which is their call to perfection. Briefly, the sincere lover wills the total order of persons and strives to encourage, insofar as he can, the growing identity of each self in its vocation to value. *Aut omnes, aut nemo.*

In order to clarify these ideas it may be useful to define more accurately the word that the problem of love obliges us to repeat over and over: "person." For the sake of simplicity we will abstract from the nuances that could be established between person and personality[1] and simply say: *personality is the condition of the self[2] that obliges it to seek its progressive fulfillment by itself, according to a perspective at once unique and universal.* This definition implies the notion of irreversible duration: each person is an historical development; at least we have no experience of a form of personality other than this. It supposes, besides, a self-creating continuity, that is, the presence of free causality in the self. And finally, it establishes the self in a vocation to totality; it recognizes in the self, by that very fact, the highest form of finality and value. The person must reach out to everything without consenting to dissipate itself in triviality or enclose itself in egoism; it is called to possess itself in order to give itself and, by this double movement, fulfills itself in an equilibrium at once mobile and continuous. In appearance a human being is only a tiny drop of psychic awareness; in reality it is a crucible wherein the spiritual universe seeks to give and receive all its energy in an irreplaceable individuality.

The real difficulty with the notion of person is that it has to be defined as a universal perspective, i.e., by the juxtaposition of two seemingly incompatible terms. How can a perspective, or individual consciousness, be total without losing its very individuality? This cannot be seen at first glance. Thus the ordinary tendency of philosophers is to classify person with bio-social individuality and regard the life of the mind as impersonal. This was, as is well known, the policy adopted by M. Brunschvicg. He used to tell me: "The farther I go, the more impersonalist I become." He would add that in formulating the *cogito* Descartes certainly had no intention of proclaiming *ego sum Cartesius*.[3]

But such a position, no matter how noble the motives, is unsatisfactory. In the first place, it conflicts with the fact that the representation of the impersonal is an eminently personal act; this representation does not make the self disappear, it purifies it by contact with objectivity and the intellectual exercise of anonymity, which is not the same thing as mere impersonality. Is it not remarkable that the strongest personalities, those whose unique character is revealed in genius, should be precisely the ones who are the least embarrassed by the conscious awareness of their best and deepest self, or by their immersion in the absolute of the spiritual life? We may find it difficult to imagine the survival of a weak individuality in the ocean of infinite truth, beauty, and goodness where it would be rudely thrown and obliged to grow; but it was in a divine milieu that Aristotle, Beethoven, and Shakespeare accentuated the traits of their original consciousness, instead of allowing them to fade away there. The imprint of their personality is deeper in proportion as their elevation is greater. The higher they are the more readily they can be discerned. If there is any conclusion to be drawn, it is that the growth of inwardness and personality, far from conflicting with each other, run a parallel course.

Finally, and above all, the reconciliation of the self and the spirit is evident as soon as one analyzes the fact of love: in it, and in it alone, we understand that the self can keep and increase its singular self-awareness by becoming universal; for the self, by loving, wills to promote other selves and reach the entire universe of the spirit through them, step by step. The very act by which the individual consciousness is determined, leads it to all things and bids it develop them, i.e., understand them and help them to understand themselves and to be. In this way the route by which we were seeking to unite the subject and the absolute, the one and the many, the individual perspective and the universe, is opened wide to us. Thus, just as the person is basically committed to love, the purpose of love is to constitute persons; it cannot will a self without having to will at the same time the other selves to keep pace with the perfection of its movement. They and it do not draw away from the spirit, and the spirit cannot withdraw from them. The unique is thus bound to totality, and totality does not destroy the multitude of unique subjects but gives them consistency.

But experience teaches us that the valorization of the self is accomplished by means of a hierarchy of physical, social, or moral processes without which the self could never awaken to its proper destiny and grow in it. From the viewpoint of love this means that it cannot carry out its program all at once in itself or others: each being and each form of being is for it so many stages on an endless road. This is why the values it pursues are fragmented and arranged in degrees. We cannot, for instance, love the Chinese except through our own countrymen, or work for the prosperity of future generations except by dedicating ourselves to our contemporaries. We have noted that the fundamental form of this dedication may be narrow and that the dyad is at every moment the receptacle in which universal cooperation must be both contained and deepened. There follows not only a segmentation of the values of love but a relative opposition between them: the farthest become the rival of the nearest. It is quite evident that the exclusive service of one of these terms would make us neglect the other; however, can a person succeed in the one without at the same time including something of the other? The end of love is always beyond the immediate task; the value it seeks is ultimately measured by the balance of its tentative and partial efforts. Nothing, therefore, prevents our maintaining our original position: love wills the total order of persons, even though it may approach it only by degrees, for no other values can satisfy here.

It remains for us to determine how love uses the means to promote each consciousness. The means are of two kinds: at one time it will be *persons* themselves who serve to love other persons, at another it is *things,* i.e., material beings or anonymous ideas. In the first instance the means should also be ends in themselves: when I use the other for the good of a third person, my act is immoral and my love contradictory if I do not respect in that living instrument a destiny as precious as that of the third party. The consciousness I call an instrument ought to be in some respect a collaborator and an equal. Things, on the contrary, are pure means; their end is projected beyond themselves into the consciousness that accepts them: they are worthy of respect only by that title, as vehicles or enrichments of personal beings.

Whether they be living or inanimate, the instrumental values love seeks will have as their role either to directly advance persons or bring them back to the level from which they may have fallen. They lend themselves to a technique of ascending progress or salvific redemption. We understand why the spirit of redemption, love's most generous invention, submits first to the exigencies of a justice that is often powerless to achieve by itself its work of retrieving the past. The love that wills the growth of the other is turned toward the future from the very outset; but redemptive love reaches it only by a return to the past which it attempts to convert and endow with new value.

IS LOVE THE SUPREME VALUE?

Were we to follow the movement of liberation and reformation at the heart of human love, we would see that it tends to sublimate itself, to unfold itself, and to reveal within itself a love that is no longer human but absolute, since it is the principle of the universal synthesis in which human love is situated. When my consciousness seeks to promote another without reserve, it discovers an infinite plan of action that it did not initiate and whose justification depends on the infinite itself. All we do is apply in a particular case of our own the cosmic desire for harmony that is proposed to our activity and gives us our vocation. Our imperfect love is rooted in a perfect order that is our autonomous model and whose value is placed above all the others, since it confers on them a definitive meaning and is presented as the value of values. From the very first it wills the infinite, not only in the manner that the true and the beautiful may will it, but still more by uniting in itself the exigencies of the true and the beautiful, for it envelopes the whole symphony of values in its own.

Love dares to aspire to the conquest and explanation of all realities: the task it assumes is to take the universe as it is and transform it according to its own law. It is the ideal that, under penalty of destroying itself, recoils before nothing. The moment it despaired of overcoming evil it would be completely annihilated. Any timidity is its ruin. It is ready to create and to destroy, to assimilate and regulate the diversity of beings. It commits itself to acquire the fullness of the real if it does not yet possess it. It is a voracious and agile value that wants to leave nothing without relation to itself and cannot rest unless it is allowed to control all destinies. It alone aspires to bear the weight of the world; indeed, it must do so by reason of its original *élan;* if it refuses, it is cut off at the root and disintegrates in contradiction.

Thus, love cannot accommodate itself to the "coordinate" role assigned to it by some thinkers: it must be all or nothing. This is where love differs so much from other values which meet an absolute limit of their power or validity, or else evaporate at a given moment of their development. I do not mean simply the utilitarian or instrumental values that bear within themselves the testimony of their subordination; even the true and the good, although they are universals and cannot be made the means of other values, are incapable of *saturating* the universe. When I have looked at all things *sub specie bonitatis* I can subsequently view them *sub specie veritatis.* . . . Love, on the contrary, contains, or summons before it, these points of view; it does not use them, it is their soul and their plenitude. They are only aspects; it is complete vision. By its essence love is the value to which no higher value can be added and to which no value can be foreign. In attributing this privileged place to it we do no injustice to the federation of values or their multiplicity of dimensions. Analysis shows that no other value can claim such primacy without diminishing the others or using them as instruments. Love alone can animate them all while respecting them all. Its determination is to be the soul of all determinations.

But the mode of relation that binds love to all ultimate values is not the same one that binds it to instrumental values nor to the various forms of concrete existence. The variety of its relationships with each being is unlimited. That is why it would be ridiculous to imagine that a metaphysics of charity could *deduce* the content of experience and the unfolding of history. Love is committed to a polymodal justification; in truth, each individuality, each idea, each fleeting trait of the universe is bound to it according to a special and unpredictable relationship. Just as mathematics is the domain of order and yet each new theorem is an original expression in that order, so, too, the bonds binding each being with love are the inexhaustible invention of an ever new relationship. The dialectic of love is constantly bursting the rigid molds in which people try to enclose it. At one time it is the principle of deduction, at another it is the rule of equilibrium, at still another it responds to the anguish of the world with a cry that overwhelms anguish and transforms it, even when it seemed beyond the possibility of transformation. Now it may show itself by a swift descent to the depths of an idea, and then it may slowly turn another one over and over. The way it deals with life is still more ingenious than its manner of combining ideas. Love fulfills some beings by gentle growth; others it breaks in order to perfect them. Its immanences are the indefinitely renewed activity of its transcendent freedom. Love is the only value that can claim *a priori* the distinction of being regarded both as the final cause of the universe and a cause strong enough to draw all the other types of causality in its wake.

Is this theoretic *pretension* a theoretic *success?* I do not deny that he who tries to justify the universe philosophically by love does so at a great risk. A perfect human interpretation of the world is impossible in a world that is itself imperfect. But it is possible to show with certitude that the promise offered by the value of love is always kept in the particular cases that the philosopher can analyze. However, for another reason it must be admitted that here the ambition exceeds the execution. This is because the philosophy of love is still at foundation level; it has scarcely advanced since Plato. Has anything in this area been systematically studied in modern times, with the possible exception of the relationships between love and knowledge or justice? Max Scheler tried to single out sympathy for special study; but do we have even a single important monograph on its relation to hatred, indifference, or severity? Kierkegaard offered some suggestions along these lines, but nothing more. The Anglo-Saxons, MacTaggart in particular, have begun to speak of its relations with the absolute. Theologians are the ones who have most closely examined the conflicts between charity and evil and their possible reconciliation. But even these regions hold unexplored secrets! Most of the attempts to discover them have been superficial; they do no more than pipe conventional tunes.

Philosophers should come to grips with this great theme instead of abandoning it to the novelists and poets. Love would go bankrupt if it could not be clarified by the reflection it provokes, and if it did not shed some light on such fraudulent imitations as are fabricated by thinkers who conspire to overthrow its eternal order with all the more temporal force as they are the more popular and united.

Should an example be needed of this masterful virtuosity that is love's privilege, let us examine how it is associated on the one hand with knowledge or will, and on the other with hate. As to the former, it is an analytic relationship; as to the latter, it is a victory over the irrational. Real knowledge is an extract of love: it wills, in its own way, the other as other. As the scholastics saw well, it has something of an altruistic character. One could comment, in this sense, on the statement of Cardinal Vital du Four: *quanto clarius intelligo, tanto ardentius diligo.* Doubtless, if the human intellect, according to St. Thomas, becomes in a certain manner all things, it is because things measure it and gratuitously communicate their form to it. But this initial subordination of our intellect only proves that the creature receives the altruistic impulse in the understanding before making it its own by the formation of concepts; the altruism of knowledge is, in a word, simultaneously a gift and an act. In this philosophy it is more completely altruistic than in subjective idealism; it is so even in the understanding of earthly things, which is inferior, discursive, and liable to end in the concept without attaining to beings. Inversely, real love contains knowledge and develops it in its depths as a germ indispensable to its own essence. In this respect, Father Rousselot transposes into philosophy a theological statement of St. Thomas: *qui plus habebit de caritate, perfectius Deum videbit.*[4] This could be denied only by substituting the impoverished forms of love for the rich ones: the *amor sensitivus* for the *amor intellectivus,* that is, by confining it to an emotional impulse, or else by reducing it to the state of an inert fruition and suppressing at the same time the possibilities it might offer for psychological and metaphysical investigation.

A similar demonstration shows the relationships between love and the will. From the very first our fundamental will thrusts us beyond ourselves toward an infinite Good, and invites us to constitute ourselves for others; no will is perfect except in being perfect love. Opinions may differ on the hierarchical order of intelligence, will, and sentiment in love, but we cannot help seeing their connection; and, truly, when one deduction opposes another too violently in this matter, it may be that the aspects of the soul are being regarded as quite separable, thus killing the living organism that penetrates them.[5]

The analysis of impartiality may illustrate the innermost character of this union. Only the impoverished forms of love are partial in the pejorative sense of this word; they cure through failure, so that one may say that disappointment becomes the principle of true knowledge. When the passions turn into indifference, truth appears. But this correctness is the point of departure, or rather the first manifestation, of a new love containing the knowledge and willing the determinations of the being known in its essential reality. Impartiality is thus the fruit of true love; it is at least its first degree. If love develops subsequently beyond this minimum, which opens to disinterested knowledge and action, it will no doubt seem to return to the attitude of partiality. That is because love will not be satisfied to place all real determinations on the same level; it espouses their best and most secret movement to dispose them according to the ideal order of the loving will in its most fervent intention. This new partiality does not have the drawbacks of the other; it is not deceitful: it simply rises to the being of the ought-to-be. The intellect and will are no longer the dupes of the heart but its associates in the service of value. And the real is not deformed but surrenders totally in the penetrating and active sympathy that now envelopes it. Reality is no longer limited to achievements, past or present. It now embraces the intellect and will subsisting in and being perfected in love. We must conclude in favor of the basic inherence of the intellect and will in love, and even of their ultimate perfection in it.

Contrariwise, there is no intrinsic connection between love and hate on the spiritual plane. No matter how often they are associated at the level of dramas of passion and instinct, such an alliance is unthinkable when one rises above mutilated experience and examines the essences of these two states. Between hatred and the will to promote the other there is a chasm that pure dialectics cannot bridge. We ask: whence the need to cause suffering to one who loves us and whom we do not love, or whom we love but who does not love us? Why the frenzy to humiliate the other and inflict struggle and defeat on him under this bitter, refined, and implacable form? No one would seriously think of cultivating hate in pursuit of a perfect love, as if hatred were a novitiate of personality or a means to its normal development. Neither can anyone maintain that in detesting the other we chastise him to make him love us, for that is true only of banal hatreds and does not constitute the most deep-seated purpose of detestation. Hatred does exist, and facts oblige us to a manner of being in it that is at once unforeseen, contingent, and scandalous. The simultaneous presence of love and knowledge or will is necessary; the co-existence of love and hatred is mysterious: it supposes a kind of mental derangement and decline having a motive and a mechanism no human mind can completely fathom. Philosophers can certainly try to discern how an absolutely good charity could cause a state of things in which hatred is possible; but they are always baffled at a certain point in their investigation and cannot see things entirely from the point of view of a supreme Providence whose action is beyond their ken. At this point philosophy must perfect itself in faith and hope. Dialectics is thus forced to supplement its deductive method of reasoning with a surrender to the infinite love it is still exploring. The connection it makes so easily elsewhere now escapes its grasp and will be found only in the sacred resources of transcendence. This science has to consent to a kind of sacrifice of its own vision if it is to continue on its course.

Where a knowledge of origins is lacking, dialectics can at least perceive a recurrence and help to correct hatred with love. It is no longer a question of deduction and analysis but ascension and homage in which evil recoils before a principle stronger than itself. The supremacy of love is certainly verified again, but it is a proof toward which we must grope our way, blindfolded. The certitude that results is strong, but it is indirect and transposed in a strange style, just as hatred and evil, too, were strange.

The principle of this last demonstration could be summarized as follows: let us suppose that hatred wanted to realize itself completely—the only way it could do so would be to constantly transform its methods and object so that finally it would attack and condemn itself, tearing at and even destroying itself. When it is akin to anger it is only too plain that it cannot last long; for it aims at suppressing the one it hates, that is, suppressing its reason for being, and by so doing aim at its own annihilation. It must therefore bind the one hating to the hated one; it must wish the eternity and perfection of the being it hates in order to become itself eternal and save its mystery. What is more, it must also will that the hated one be as generous as possible in order to be itself fully gratuitous and perverse; it must ennoble its enemy and make him its benefactor and god. It is thus immediately vitiated by a contradiction that disfigures and bruises it; it must work lovingly for this god and be his servant so as to succeed in hating him more, like the wicked angel of the Old Testament who had to get his orders from the Lord before he could tempt the just ones of the earth. But hate is thus limited to a formal attitude and deliberately deprives itself of all effectiveness in order to save the insignificant domain of its intention.

Nothing prevents hatred in a free being from resting in this strange defeat as in a victory. But by resisting its enemy in the very act in which it asks him to please raise it morally, its challenge is a weakness and its effort a sham. Hatred diminishes in proportion as it attempts to realize itself. What alternative is left for it but to regain a little substance? None, no doubt, except to shift the position of its revolt and blame its god for the ontological depression in which it is struggling. In this perverse and gratuitous hatred it can escape a mortal anemia only by accusing the Other of having tried to destroy its spiritual value. The accusation then takes on a tragic grandeur and everyone knows that we do not really pardon a person whom we suspect of having degraded us; it is no longer a being full of goodness that we oppose but an evil and pernicious one. Thus the one whom we regarded a moment ago as clothed with love, we now decide to identify with the principle of evil. Hatred denies itself. However, if it regards love as detestable, it is guilty of a grave error and it knows it; so it decides to blind itself—and then where is the enlightened will that animates every serious hatred? Besides, this lie, dangerous for itself and ineffectual as regards the hated being, draws the hating one to demand his right in the name of the justice and love of which he pretends to have been defrauded. But this is a new and decisive failure, for the malicious person reintroduces in his act the cult of the moral values he had undertaken to deny. The diabolic scheme, in short, falls to pieces under its own blows, and can subsist only by never completely willing itself, that is, by trying to fix itself on shifting sands. The person who hates decides to enclose himself within limits he must will and not will at the same time. He has no alternative but to take pleasure in his own failure; and when he does, hate is dislodged and begins again its interminable, infernal dance, for the pleasure in question can no longer be that of pure hatred; it is already an intrusion of the power of loving in the very orneriness of the rebellious spirit; it is a homage his vice must render to virtue.

The loving will respects this stubbornness, however, by penetrating it with its peaceful victory; for while love makes us face ourselves involuntarily, it does no violence to us in the development it impels us to foster in ourselves voluntarily, once we are brought face to face with ourselves. But if the hate-filled spirit of revolt, wearied of itself, finally allows its iciness to melt before the fires of grace, if the rebellious will is vanquished by suffering and humility, we have a feeling that its conversion will be for it the beginning of a new series of metamorphoses. Reversing its aim one last time, hatred subsequently directs itself against hatred and its odyssey ends in repentance. Love, as the evil genius and death of death, encounters it and gently draws the self out of the morass in which it had fallen, no longer allowing it to cast itself against anyone, no matter how wicked, even should he be wickedness in person; for hatred can no longer direct its blows against anything but the self's culpable idea and evil mask. Hate bids the self destroy the reality of the evil, allowing it to perpetuate only the memory of it so as to shrink from it in an esthetic revulsion or find in it a stimulus for good. From the former fault there then proceeds an innocent and unprecedented youth. The fall from which the sinner rises is productive of good; he finds himself rewarded, as if love wanted to compensate for the former ugliness by the introduction of a new kind of beauty.

A chain of events of this kind shows us how unlimited are the means to self-fulfillment at the disposal of love's universal synthesis. Although at times we may lack direct light to help us follow its course, we do not doubt that it can always continue on its way and arrive at its goal, even while respecting vagrant freedoms. Viewed from any angle, the value of love convinces us of its supreme power in face of the world and invites us to reassess this world at all levels of existence and according to all the procedures available to the mind.

This immense program meets with a final difficulty. Is it its own value that love wills? Is it not rather the value of the person? Does it not subordinate itself to the promotion of freedoms? And hence should one not say that the supreme value is not love but personal freedom? The true end would then seem to be the fulfillment of the consciousness, freed of its tutors and open to an independent destiny.

But a twofold reply can be made to the objection. First, love does not will free personality for the sake of its freedom; it wills freedom because it is the condition of a truly loving personality. It penetrates the person with love. And then love penetrates our abstract notion of love with personality: not only does it express itself in the spiritual society of centers of consciousness but, what is more, it can be the supreme value only if it is itself a super-personality. This last thesis is equivalent to maintaining that love is the essence of God and that in it all the divine attributes are reconciled. Such an assertion is difficult to prove entirely by the sole effort of a philosophy that refuses to have recourse to the teachings of supernatural revelation. Nevertheless, reason has an intuition that love would stop midway and be irrational if it were not itself a living consciousness in which our own personality finds its source, its support, and its end. There is nothing that forbids this assertion, and all the data of our experience urge us to accept it.

IS LOVE THE SUPREME REALITY?

Love appears to us as the highest of values and its purpose is to assume in itself all reality, to the point that it justifies reality's existence by the vocation it confers on it. But what degree of reality does this purpose have? Is it positively accomplished? Is the exigency of absolute synthesis eternally satisfied? In short, does the reality of this value ever completely catch up with the reality of existence?

If we limit ourself to what the temporal order offers us visibly in the human spectacle, it would seem we should have to answer in the negative. The final cause remains beyond the world, in the realm of the possible. Pure love is a spirit which soars above facts, and the light it sheds on them is refracted in disparate colors. Absolute love is subdivided into a host of relative forms as soon as it touches our earth, and its forms sometimes clash. N. Hartmann, for example, places the love of those nearest to us at the bottom of the scale, then the love of those more distant, then the generosity emanating from the radiant person; he does not always pronounce clearly on the hierarchy of these values, but he thinks it is possible to affirm that personal love, properly so-called, should be placed above them.[6] Now, does one not serve one of these loves at the expense of the others? We alluded above to one of these conflicts, the rivalry between devotion to the nearest and devotion to the more remote; we showed that it is not unsolvable, but in practice it certainly is the cause of delicate cases of conscience. It is not easy to know when it is permitted to die oneself or take the life of another for future humanity. . . .

What is still more serious is that the ideal, even fragmented and obscure, penetrates very slowly into the reality in which our lifetime struggle is carried on. In its works *ad extra,* in the film of mundane history, love seems so weak! Its essential demands keep it far removed from the program of life as announced. Are proofs necessary? Let us examine the humblest dyad at the very beginning of the act that incarnates the ideal in observable facts. Love desires the influence of one consciousness on another. This ambition is never totally illusory, but its realization is often infinitesimal. Is it not often hopelessly optimistic to believe that the *I* can change the *thou* or even change itself for the sake of the *thou?* "Every choice has already been made," says Alain; what we imagine to be a free metamorphosis of beings is ordinarily only the implacable turning of their mechanism. Besides, human reciprocities are weak, and when autonomy asserts itself, even if it is nurtured in the goodness of the other, it turns away from the mother-soul and fulfills itself in revolt.

However, so much emphasis is placed today on that somber aspect of the question that in the end the facts are often exaggerated and distorted. Perception of others and reciprocal influences are real; and sometimes they even really attain their maximum. Lovers are not deceived in this: they know very well that they are bound by a mutual gift. If in the *Satin Slipper,* Rodrigue and Prouhèze were mistaken in this regard, the whole atmosphere of the drama would be changed. Similarly, were I not loath to demean the discussion by a coarse reflection, I would say with Marcel Proust: "The husbands who are deceived and know nothing know everything just the same." This is also true outside the pages of literature: life testifies in this sense when it renounces its passionate prejudices and consents to recollect itself and listen to the sincere voice speaking within. We have to insist that reciprocal knowledge, despite its blunders, is very often true, and everyone is, deep down, convinced of this. The skeptics, when they stop writing books and seriously face the *other,* are just as convinced as the rest.

In a certain psychology that passes for realistic, it is good form to pretend that the successes of human love are owing to the imagination and that we never either know or change another being. "Love is nothing but a hypothesis changed into a fixed idea," P. Janet teaches; "the person we love will be credited with having the power to console us when we are sad, restore our courage when we are weak, point out the path of life, and generally help us. He really does not have this power at all; he does not dream of having it; he is incapable of having it; but that makes no difference. We pretend he is this kind of person. This is what constitutes love."[7]

The cynicism of the last sentence does not do away with the enigma presented by the facts, and it masks the rarest and most precious part of it. That the mind should be able to feed only on vapor is, on reflection, the strangest of mysteries. Even if reciprocity is only a double illusion, there is absolutely no proof that the agreement of two illusions is itself an illusion. That agreement is perceptible and sometimes maintained by a double consent is what keeps a spark of truth alive in the most pitiful attachments. But we must go farther. Is it so disastrous that imagination should be an integral part of love? People vilify the loving imagination without noticing that, granting a certain discipline, it can become a positive factor in the success of love. What they call illusion is perhaps quite simply an anticipation. This it is that binds the past state of the lovers to their future; it is by this that they can model each other according to an ideal. Without the image they would be unable to pass from contemplation to action. It is thanks to it that the popular antinomy of love can further be resolved: it is blind, they say, and yet it reveals. Blind to what limits and deforms, it reveals what develops and reforms. Such, at least, is love's role in a consciousness capable of escaping the equivocal enchantments of any kind of intermediary and bending itself to a spiritual purpose. Far from leading us necessarily into error and solitude, the imagination can lead us to a fine perception and mutual fulfillment that is far from mythical.

But no matter what the successes of human love may be, they are episodic and partial. They are springtimes between two winters; summer is not for this world. And so these successes alone do not allow us to conclude to the reality of a divine Providence whose plan would always be favorable to us and include the whole world. We arrive at that kind of conviction by other roads, and in particular by philosophical reflection on the origin and consistency of persons, independently even of their earthly supports. These inquiries are not our subject. Thus it would be intellectually foolhardy to claim at this point to have proved that an absolute and eternal Goodness really does direct the total cosmic reality. Certainly nothing prevents an infinite and supreme Will from being entirely perceptible in a limited experience. However, it is a fact that this transcription has not yet been achieved in our world. Love is the highest and most demanding value—that is certain. Is it also the supreme reality and the master obeyed by every other reality? What we have said does not give an absolutely precise knowledge of it, but it does permit us to believe it, and in affirming it, to choose wisely. To reflect on the implications of human love is to dispose oneself, if not to see God, at least to believe in Him; it is to discover something of His essence, if not of His existence. The phenomenon of human reciprocities, feeble though it be, draws us far above ourselves and allows us to catch a glimpse of the fact that every being is already subject to an ever vigilant and victorious Charity.

NOTES

1. In *La Réciprocité des consciences. Essai sur la nature de la personne* (Paris: Aubier, 1942), I limit the word "person" to the spirit that animates and stirs all personalities into being; in other words, to the divinity itself. For the moment I shall ignore this distinction and speak only of human subjects.

2. A more explicit analysis would also require a further definition of "self," "I," and "subject."

3. R. Lenoble has taken up the challenge and proposed a personalist exegesis of Cartesianism that sacrifices none of the prerogatives of the mind. See his book on the *Notion d'expérience* (Paris, 1942); also G. Lewis' work: *L'Individualité selon Descartes* (Paris, 1950). One day, as I was arguing the point with M. Brunschvicg, I asked

him: "Don't you see any way to save the person? According to your view can't it escape from the shipwreck of the substance of the realist?" He answered by expounding a theory on the function of personalization that I found very simply and clearly stated again in his posthumous work, *Héritage de mots, héritage d'idées* (Paris, 1945, p. 71): "Man will have access to his soul only by the exercise of a personalizing function which of itself is in no way limited to the horizon of his individuality . . . but is capable of making one's self and that of the other communicate interiorly, or better still, which substitutes the limitless comprehension and generous expansion of the Cartesian *cogito* in us for the realist's impenetrable self."

The concession should not be overlooked; but it does not in any way constitute a retraction, and I should not wish to take unfair advantage of it.

4. P. Rousselot, "Synthèse aperceptive et philosophique de l'amour," *Revue de Philosophie,* March 1, 1910. The article begins with the double thesis: "The perfect intelligible is a living spirit; perfect knowledge is identical with love." I find less satisfying the book by the same author on the *Problème philosophique de l'amour au Moyen-Age* (2nd ed., Paris, 1932). The first doctrine he considers there, and which he calls Greco-Thomist, insists on the relation of the part to the whole. The part, we are told, ought to be ready to sacrifice itself for the whole, for it loves itself more and better in it than it would apart from it; it is naturally ordered to the whole. Thus, according to Aristotle's example, the hand raises itself to the face to defend the body against danger. The idea is profound, but it does not sufficiently distinguish between the relations of nature and the relations of persons. A certain uneasiness results, and the analysis seems incomplete: it keeps us within Aristotelian limits, perhaps, and certainly within Thomistic ones, while commenting on them. Etienne Gilson rightly points out that in Thomism, when it is a question of the love of man for God, man is not a *part* but an *image* of God, which is quite different. "For a being who resembles God," Gilson adds, "the more he resembles Him, the more faithful he is to himself." (*L'Esprit de la philosophie médiévale,* Paris, 1932, II, 93; English translation by A. H. C. Downes, *The Spirit of Medieval Philosophy,* London: Sheed and Ward, 1936, p. 302.) Indeed, the relation of one consciousness to another is never that of a fragment to a whole or even of an organ to the body.

The second section deals with the doctrine that P. Rousselot calls "ecstatic," and which is said to have been cultivated especially by the Franciscan school. It supposes: first, the duality of the lover and the beloved; second, the violence of love (i.e., its incapacity for realizing itself without destroying the self of the lover); third, an irrational movement; fourth, the character of final end attributed to love. This second doctrine examines personal relationships more fully, but it is at times arbitrarily imposed by the author on a number of divergent writings which he seems to adapt by force to his over-all plan. I, for my part, would accept the first and fourth points but not the other two.

Echoing the quarrels of the Middle Ages are those of the seventeenth and eighteenth centuries on pure love. I shall say nothing about them in the present essay; but the reader will not find it difficult, I suppose, to guess that, while admiring the psychological penetration and loftiness of Fénelon's views, I would side more than once, almost regretfully, with Bossuet or Malebranche, and especially Leibniz. *Magis amica veritas....*

5. Similar reflection might guide us in the analysis of the bond that binds together love and truth, love and sincerity, etc., with the nuances that theory and practice suggest in each instance.

6. *Ethics,* 3 vols, translated by Stanton Colt (New York, Humanities, 1932).

7. *Evolution psychologique de la personnalité* (Paris, 1930), pp. 332-3.

II ✧ The Continuity of Centers of Consciousness

4 ❖ The Data of Consciousness and the Gift of Persons

The problem of human knowledge is logically bound up with the problem of person. Kant brooded over the former and was soon drawn toward the latter. Since Kant, however, this connection has often been misunderstood. Philosophers have tended to limit themselves to the point of departure of critical analysis, which was the perception of matter, and have tried to include in it the total relation of subject to object. Consequently the study of interpersonal knowledge has remained in the shadow; this was the initial mutilation of the problem of knowledge. There was another: the relation of consciousness to nature suffered in its turn from the excessive attention given to sensible intentionality; for by dint of being occupied with things, consciousness ended by losing sight of the fact that itself was not a thing.

And so philosophers of the person had best rethink the whole epistemological problem. They are well prepared to do so. Instead of posing stiffly on the periphery of conscious-

85

ness in a kind of neutral zone, where they can abstract from the knowing subject, they now proceed by way of reflection on the subject himself and thus derive more than one valuable clue not only to the nature of the subject's knowledge but also to the beings that he contacts.

When I reflect on the act of my knowledge and want to describe it, one of the fundamental notions that immediately rises in my mind is that of *datum*. What is a datum? Language designates ordinarily by this word all that is thrust at or proposed to me immediately, i.e., whatever I receive simply and without reasoning or at least what is so elemental that, far from being hampered by my subsequent reasonings, will be confirmed by them. The datum is an interior thing that criticism cannot touch. Besides, it is understood that it bears witness to its own reality: it is a presentation and not a representation. Even if it is a distorted image or a chimera, it inevitably implies a certain form of existence whose claims we may have to clarify or correct, but which cannot be entirely stripped of the titles it sometimes greedily assumes.

Thus limited, the term still remains, it must be admitted, quite vague and heterogeneous. Perhaps it will become clearer if we examine its principal forms that in a provisory and somewhat sibylline fashion I will call obstacle-datum, gift-datum, and giver-datum.

The *obstacle-datum* is what I encounter on my way without my inner self's being enriched thereby or even respected. The enchantment of nature interrupts my being like an intruder; even though it constantly accompanies my *cogito,* it is both strange and a stranger to me. I can no more identify with it than a prisoner can identify with the walls of his cell. What surprises the self above all in this world is the revelation that it constantly has of a counter-reality that undoes it, or at least overflows and threatens, even while seeming to support it. Between a chair and myself, between a landscape and myself, the initial relationship for me is that of a pure discovery: I find the chair, I am confronted by the landscape as if I were standing before something extraneous to my essence and existence, something that does not enter into their circle and that no finality intrinsically orientates toward me at the moment of our encounter. I cannot deduce the sensible data, I cannot simply assume them as if they were aspects of myself of which I am unaware. Perhaps I shall have to try to do so subsequently, but before I do try, these data are presented to me as superfluous to my being. And their very superfluity stifles, paralyzes, or dangerously charms me, in short, empties me of a presence which was myself, only to cast me into the disturbing multitude of a non-self.

The obstacle-datum did not will me, and at first I scarcely will its presence: we have met by pure chance, that is, without sufficient reason, without definite promise, through the effect of an unforeseeable juxtaposition. The rock that I perceive yonder can crush me or become my shelter: it will serve or disserve my insertion in the world; but originally it is neuter, it is itself; it is not *I* nor is it for *me;* it is neither *in* me nor *of* me. Perhaps the best formula I have to express my grasp of it would be: I am aware that it is with me. But in that coincidence there remains a gap in space and in time: in space, for where the obstacle-datum sometimes appears to me, it is always at a distance from me; and in time, for whenever it appears to me it rises out of a past that has totally shaped its presence and separates it from my present. The space-time interval that makes us parallel prevents us from being fraternal: it is precisely because it is with me in this way that the datum disrupts my continuity and, while revealing a non-self to me, begins by attacking my self.

There are, of course, degrees in the exteriority of the obstacle-datum. The scintillation of a star or the verdure of a lawn are farther removed from me than the beating of my heart. External nature disconcerts me more than my body. In themselves these data of whatever type contain a call to a different objectivation. Doubtless none of my senses is particularly reserved to any one of these types, for all of the senses have, at the outset, a cosmic and organic reach. But in each one of the senses certain data tell me more about the world than about my body, and others reveal my body more than the world. The whole cosmos as sensed is, as it were, my body; and the whole organism can be sensed as a cosmos. It is nevertheless certain that the shining of the star resolves the ambiguity of my sensitive life in a manner opposed to the interiority that my heartbeat brings to me. Thus, before any conceptualization, there are two distinct degrees, or two forms, of obstacle data.

Finally, there is a third obstacle, closer to me than the world, closer to me than my body itself, and yet irreducible to my personal act: the psychic zone that surrounds, precedes, or follows me. It is made up of my impulsive movements and my apathies. There I find my temperament and my habits— my childish dissipation and also the retreats of my mind in a kind of shelter of nameless qualities. This self that gropes about and gets lost is not my self, but sometimes comes close to being so, or may have once been so; it is not yet in the space-time of my body and corporal *Umwelt;* but it is already in a kind of virtual extension and, in any case, in a temporary disconnection that separates it from my subjectivity itself.

The kind of obstacle that we thus are to ourselves is nonetheless instructive. By it we know that man retains something of the ape and that the conscious person is exposed to the infantile competition of an unconscious psyche. Above all, we know we are exposed to the vertigo of abdication or alienation: we can lose ourselves in a kind of objective splitting of the personality and devaluate the self in the non-self, betraying our essence, at least in part. We have the mysterious power to exile ourselves and pass over, bag and baggage, into the vast community of impersonal beings. The gnostics used to imagine that particles of a luminous kingdom had been deported and shut up in a kingdom of shadows. This hypothesis is not entirely false, since self-alienation is a fact. It may be that the alienated self is not irremediably lost and that its captivity is not a radical metamorphosis or a regressive evolution.

But while waiting to be redeemed, the alienated self sees itself as an impenetrable, insupportable block. Instead of transcending itself it feels transcended by its own refusal to transcend. Henceforth it no longer recognizes itself but clashes with substitutes for itself that seem to be transcendent. In short, the mind that flees from itself can cease to recognize the fact; it is doubtless at this moment that it sets up the idol of its own defection and adores it in terror. In the obstacle offered to us in this form we have the origin of all idols and false otherness that only aggravate our loneliness.

Quite other is the *gift datum.* This is the name we can give to what comes to us not only as anticipation of our hopes but also as a rich endowment of our personal being. This is particularly true of those absolute values we call goodness, beauty, and truth. There is nothing threatening about them. Rather, they speak to us of a Baudelairian land where all is *"luxe, calme et volupté."* Although values are not perceived except in a human act and an incipient work, they are offered to us as from a fountain whose source is not in us, for all poetry is a gift of the gods, all moral progress a gift of grace, and all truth an illumination of the mind. In every respect their essence is oblative: these values respond to the scarcely formulated desire of our being and contain the ideal form of the event or element on which they rest; they are diffused like an act of generosity so pristine that they seem to be a gift without a giver and a spring without a source. Finally, whereas the obstacle was distance and delay, value is inwardness and anticipation; it restores the rhythm that nature allows to fade.

We are quite aware that such a theory of value invites sarcasm and is apt to be regarded as medieval naivete or a Platonic relic. But while it may not satisfy contemporary philosophers, it is at least necessarily implied in the spontaneous state of soul of the greatest spiritual geniuses. This testimony certainly has its value. The only possible objection to it would be that the first impression may be deceptive: who knows whether the growth of values will not, on the one hand, devour persons and, on the other, stir up conflict in values themselves? We reply that the bond between value and personal masterpieces suffices to show its unlimited tolerance for human development. Value teaches us to always surpass ourselves, and this is also what personal fulfillment demands. As for rivalry among values, even if it poses the agonizing problem of the compatibility of causes, it does not engender conflict except as a consequence of the inchoate or impure perception of values. *Ueber allen Gipfeln ist Ruhe.* In other words, the deeper our knowledge of value is, the less we risk being diminished or divided by it, or setting it against itself. The incompatibilities of the values disappear as the values grow. Their supposed misdemeanors are only accidents of our spiritual adolescence.

But is it really certain that the datum of value is not simply a particular group of the natural data that we were examining above? One might indeed hesitate if the domain of value were restricted to a determined portion of experience. But this is not the case: everything can be contemplated under the ideal aspect. The broadest value, and, in a sense, the only value, is the beautiful, provided one gives that word all the authority and fullness it often loses in contemporary language. For is not truth the compelling beauty of relationships, and is not goodness the beauty of behavior?[1] Consequently, by affirming that all things can be regarded ideally, we are saying that all things have an esthetic end. A conflagration or a crime may be palliated only in an artist's conscience; it would be odious to maintain that their empiric being contains their beauty. Beauty descends upon their being and does not result from it. That is why we refused to identify obstacle-datum with value-datum. The first asserts itself upon contact with another thing; the second is above all things and for all things. To this difference are related others we have already implicitly indicated: data of the first type isolate consciousness; data of the second bring to it a fellowship or at least a semi-fellowship; if the first type removes us from our natural element by space-time dispersion, the second arrests this dispersion and elevates the world toward a kind of eternity.

The datum may be a gift identified with the giver.

We believe this to be so each time there is perception of a person, for the person is not accessible unless he gives himself in a certain manner to the one who beholds him. This is why we believed it possible to sustain a series of apparently paradoxical theses whose principles are as follows: every perception of the other implies a minimum of reciprocity; every reciprocity is initially and essentially allied to love; all personal love is at one and the same time feeling, knowledge, and will to promote the self of the other; finally, every will to promotion involves a continuity of the world of spirits and even a heterogeneous identity of the *I* and *thou,* since the ideal *I* and *thou* are then one in the loving act. Thus the problem of the perception of the other can, characteristically, be clarified only in the light of a metaphysics of love, for this alone can make the relation between the one and the many in the spiritual world intelligible.[2]

We cannot here develop these affirmations nor show how they can be reconciled with the partial ineffectiveness of love or with the fact that the *imperium* of the lover, if it is effective, will stimulate the freedom of the beloved whose autonomy is quite different from the separated existence nature opposes to us. At the level of inter-human psychology the themes we would meet on this subject are the ones that formerly occupied the theology of grace and freedom. Could it be that by transposing them we would reunite them? The personal datum is not wholly contained in the single relation that binds me to the other and presupposes our radical existence as persons; it is also contained in that radical existence itself whose fundamental mystery, whose source is in God, our mutual influences do not penetrate. By becoming aware of myself I really become aware that my very *cogito* is given to me: I think, therefore I am thought (someone thinks me); I am, i.e., I am willed. But to designate the giver in the gift of my constitutive act and to assure me that he is a living Creator rather than an anonymous value, would call for a dialectic leading us far beyond the initial psychological fact of human reciprocity where we started. It is to this we must now return in order to examine how in this case the *datum* is a *donor*.

First of all, the awareness of my being reveals to me that I have debts to others besides myself. If solipsism is absurd, it is because the concrete grasp of my act is at the same time the intuition of human influences that have helped promote me since the cradle: neither revolt nor the fiction of my isolation can free me from this condition. I cannot deny others without denying myself. Doubtless I have only a general view of my history and the attention I give to the past of others in me will have varying degrees. It is even true that I can bring emphasis to bear on one aspect more than another and that ordinarily I observe myself more attentively than I do others. But the free activity connected with the utilization of data does not attenuate in the least the fact that my being has two sides and that the act by which I am is the very act by which someone causes me to be. The autonomy I give myself is ontologically proportionate to the presences I have received. A similar observation could be made with reference to the relation between my existence and what other existences have become as a consequence of mine.

It may be objected that these virtual presences are very close to being absences. This we deny. The perception of others is almost always repressed, forgotten, or distorted; but its first movement is and always will be immaculate. In this first movement, which represents the indestructible minimum of reciprocity, the perceiving subject ratifies and extends the being of the subject perceived. He can know it only by increasing the community of their initial encounter, and that encounter is simultaneously the work of both: the one perceived is perceived only because he is a person offered to the world; the one perceiving perceives only by accepting that offer, i.e., by actualizing it in a new sense, as a musician imposes a variation on a theme given to him which modifies both the being of the theme and his being as a musician. Born in this circuit, other-perception aims spontaneously at widening and vivifying it. It tends toward a dialogue in which each person returns to his partner the gift he receives from him after stamping his mark on it. Mutual causality ceaselessly alters and amplifies a process that is a creation of self by self, thanks to a creation of self by the other. It succeeds in uniting apparently divergent notions of initiative, influence, and community. It is, in a word, the only example at our disposal for understanding the coincidence of being and freedom, or of the same and the other.

If, therefore, the perception of persons were actualized according to the very first orientation of its movement, reciprocity would be perfectly loving and liberating. This is evidently not the case. Experience shows us that no one advances very far on this attractive but steep road. Humanity, victim of a strange psychological catastrophe, glimpses the communion of centers of consciousness only to turn away from it. Hatred, pettiness, and indifference stop and immediately reverse this creative vision, a vision that ordinarily only poets prize as something about which to write, and only saints adopt as something by which to live.

What is more, we use the initial grace of the glance the better to kill and degrade its object. Indeed, the most disquieting aspect of diabolic inversion is that it always has to begin by devouring the flesh of angels. The spiritual loss of the world that terrified Port-Royal is an undeniable fact. We do not mean to deny that the course of reciprocity and its actualization involve a host of obligatory and optional halts that compromise the journey. Our purpose is to show that at the outset there is present a datum uniting the subject in a vocation to be donors. This primary fact is not laid down by faith and hope but by experience and reason. It has been strangely disregarded to the great detriment of the theory of knowledge and the metaphysics of the person.

Even in the shipwreck of reciprocity and the unleashing of contradictory passions, the world keeps some spiritual islands that still express, under unexpected forms, the radical structure of the collegiality of persons. It is observed, for example, in certain cases of unhappy love that are not superficial caprices but tragic and operative trials. At this level, to which an implacable law demands that one accede only at the price of tears and blood, the will to fulfillment seeks gropingly and discovers at last the most personal form of the loved *thou,* both as an ideal to be brought to victory and as the most real being of the other: for the true ideal is nothing but the right of a dazzling reality to transmute all that is not yet itself. At this precise moment the two beings suddenly coincide in what is best and most unique in their possession: the will of the loving self creates and constitutes the most irreplaceable will of the *thou* it loves. But in the same indivisible movement the *I* that promotes the *thou* finds its own perfect uniqueness. It receives what it gives. That is why, even in the case in which the empirical response of the beloved is ridiculously inadequate, the heroic lover is still above the frailties of the beloved and the blows of a rival: he holds the secret of a *thou* who is more *thou* than the other aspects of the beloved and is forever inviolable. He has unearthed a virtual soul which is stifling, yet will never die, even if it never triumphs. This virtual soul is an eternal protest; it is the truest of all the images of the other. In this sense, the gift, which often has its bitterness, always has its reward. It prolongs the example of the One of whom Pascal has remarked: "I am more a friend to you than this or that one . . . I love you more ardently than you loved your blemishes." This is what explains the mysterious dignity radiating from the gift, even in the courtyard of the praetorium and on Golgotha.

Our attempt at a triple description of datum appears at first to be empiric. However, while assuming the viewpoint of the person and noting what is hostile or favorable to him, we did not act like the botanist who classifies all mushrooms as edible or poisonous. We were faced with a problem in which we ourselves were implicated: how could we have changed our post of observation without obscuring what was to be observed? As it happened, the diversity of the content of the datum clarified its diversity of form. Besides, what was empirical in the description was quickly dispelled by the universality of the question at stake. Indeed, it envelops a whole theory of knowledge.

Is our theory, as we proposed it, realistic or idealistic? It could be called realistic in that it concerns things, and idealistic in that it concerns values and persons. To be sure of this, one would have to be quite clear as to the meaning given the words. But the quarrel of idealism and realism is one of the most deceptive of all because of the incurable ambiguity of the terms. It is quite puerile for the realist to pretend that all the partisans of the opposite thesis must logically end up with solipsism; or, inversely, for the idealist to maintain that all nonidealists must be fundamentally "naive realists." These arguments *in terrorem* have never touched the really great thinkers, but they have been nourishing the philosophical chronicle for so long that they have finally tired everyone except a few grammarians. The present generation is turning away from a sterile debate so devoid of interest. I touch on it here only to assert the right to make some distinctions.

Realism is usually defined as the doctrine according to which reality is independent of the subject who knows it and is not affected by the knowledge had of it. But the idealist blithely retorts that it is impossible to directly verify this double thesis—it would require the suicide of the thinker to do so; even then, by definition, he would not succeed.[3] One is forced to fall back on the criterion of mental coherence proposed by the idealist method. Thence, between the two adversaries, chastened by their mutual attacks, there remains only a verbal distance. In effect, the idealist, for his part, will have to explain the datum, recognizing in it a set of conditions without which he could not complete his thought; this, in turn, inevitably reintroduces an intentionality of knowledge. He will thus become a reflective realist, forced to admit there is no philosophy without an order that goes beyond our strict individuality. Fundamentally, in the generation of the intelligible, realism is a doctrine and idealism a method.[4]

In any case, the dialogue can begin again and even go on forever. Instead of engaging in it, we prefer to define the obstacle-datum not as the being of which we are not the sufficient cause but as the being which is not our sufficient cause and which is even rather our deficient cause. We thus reverse the customary manner of proceeding—but at least we gain by remaining on a terrain where it is easier to know what one is talking about. To maintain that natural reality is what the subject has not made is one of the surest ways of leading realism toward a logical impasse. It will steer clear of it only if exterior reality is defined by its inability to account for our subjectivity. At the heart of the datum of encounter that nature offers us there seems to be an inevitable ambiguity and consequently a radical threat to us. Now, is nature independent of us because no ultimate solidarity binds its being to ours? At the level of perception we have no means of settling, once and for all, problems like this that would make theologians tremble. We can only observe that nature does not harmonize with our present being and that in this sense alone is it surely independent of it. Does nature then remain unaffected by the knowledge we have of it? That is incredible, for all knowledge is a grasp and a transformation. It is not indifferent to the being of the tree that I know the tree, i.e., that I step back from it and judge it to be of a different order from myself. This may have as a consequence that I will cut it down or burn it, and if it falls, I will get out of the way.

If the sensible datum is, according to the prince of realists, the common act of the one feeling and the one felt, it is the one feeling who has the lion's share in this affair. He is the one who gives flowers their bloom and tint; he is the one who draws the *"fundamentum in re"* out of its inaccessible night and lowly condition. To know things is to raise them to ourselves, even while we judge them to be contrary to ourselves and bemoan their sway over us. Because we can raise them to our level and even completely transform them as Orpheus did, the datum directs us to a point beyond itself. Objectivity tends, then, to be divided into a percept that enlightens our knowledge, and an obscure reality whose bare existence is all we know, but a datum still, and fraught with the unknown.

This knowledge that links us with nature is not exactly what an unqualified "realism" would propose. Passing now to the two other forms of data already pointed out, i.e., the *gift* of values and the *giver* of them, we may say, by way of contrast, that they are not best explained by an unmixed "idealism." Doubtless there is an affinity between the soul and values, and especially an implication of the other in the self, that seems to authorize the philosopher's dream of a universal deduction. But the exigency of a world of spirits immanent in our spirit is only the epitome of an experience in which we were willed in time before we ourselves could will and in order that we should do so. For we make ourselves in response to the appeals and challenges that define our vocation that is at once unique and universal. Some will call this "spiritual realism," and they will not be wrong.

Ours is a world of unforeseeable acts and constant exchanges in which perception is never our work alone but the result of an interaction of subjects. Insofar as we are creatures and human subjects, we are all preceded by the reality of our God and precede one another only secondarily in the being in which He constituted us.

Now, in the interplay of free beings, acceptance has as much dignity as offering. Far from being passive, the being that is received from the other is the active birth of a self-affirmation. To the idealism of a self that constitutes itself and wills to engender the universe, it would seem that a personalist philosophy must, at the outset, attach a realism of acceptance. There is no contradiction between consenting to the being and inventing it in love.[5]

There is a final reason for rejecting the idealist label in that the person always comes to us through nature. Spirit ends by touching spirit, but it begins on the road of bodies and the animal soul. It is originally subject to what it must ultimately master. It is diffused in the discontinuity of things in order to integrate it into the continuity of centers of consciousness; although the collegiality of persons does not analytically contain the concrete order of things, it does traverse it, and this association characterizes the adventure of a spiritual existence in this world. Thus we should not be surprised that spiritual perception does not inevitably coincide with the moments of sensible intensity in which it is cloaked; for the datum par excellence of the person is not his empirical character but his vocation. Man is the being that is unified in this very tension and attains its goal only by a detour through obstacles.

To conclude, we do not believe in the least that the creation of self by self, this God-given grandeur of man, demands the suppression of all philosophical first principles. Life cannot do without something having been originally given; neither can philosophy. But what is given must be interpreted, and not made an excuse for a lazy decline in spiritual vitality. Everything, in effect, is offered to us to be recreated, whether it be the obstacle of nature below or the inpouring of God above. This is what the "idealist" philosophers have clearly seen.

But in a complementary sense this reaction makes us face the necessity in us of something that is given and regard self-creation as simply derived from the exigency of our very being. By reflecting we learn that reflection is not everything and needs spontaneity. In the Christian Trinity the gift of the Father does not diminish the dignity of the Son. Much more, the gift of God, or the gift of the other, or the gift of bodies should not offend the created person whose subtle nobility implies humility too. And this is what the realist thinkers would have us remember. The first deduction of spiritual exigency is that not everything can be deduced, but everything can be respected so that it can be redeemed. Thus we are afforded a glimpse of how the data of consciousness are assumed in the communion of persons.

NOTES

1. Thus the ancient doctrine of transcendentals might be extended without contradiction, for beauty thus understood is rational and expresses being.

2. See my *Réciprocité des consciences* (Paris, 1942) and *La Personne humaine et la nature* (Paris, 1943).

3. Likewise, the independence and inviolability of being with relation to the thinker are equivocal notions: they designate at one time the plurality of elements distributed haphazardly in the calculation of probabilities and at another the autonomy of a subject that is willed by another subject in the interpersonal relationship, i.e., a limitation; or, on the contrary, a gift made to the intellect, i.e., a liberation. In speaking thus of a reality independent of us and coming in contact with us, we use a uniform vocabulary for heterogeneous experiences.

4. Cf. P. Guérin, *Certitudes morales* (Strasbourg, 1946).

5. The reception of things is itself an act; but hampered by their passivity, this act is inferior to that of spiritual association.

5 ✦ *The Meaning of the Ideal Self*

All life is metamorphosis, but the metamorphosis of human consciousness is accompanied by a special image, that of the ideal self. In all the changes I will, it is a new selfhood I seek. I project on the road a shadow of my person that I perpetually strive to reach and that is always just ahead of me.

Doubtless the ideal self often seems to fade before the brilliance of the objects I perceive or to yield under the pressure of the projects I am constructing. But this withdrawal is not an absence; it is the diffusion of a presence that, for all its unobtrusiveness, is none the less real and indispensable. It only teaches me that the image of my ideal self is not like other images and that I ought rather to conceive it as a source or vehicle of images.

There is no denying that the ideal self is an imperfect, equivocal, and unstable frame of reference for conscious life. That is why philosophy has often turned away from it with the uneasiness one feels before vague notions whose form and content seem too shadowy and shifting. This disfavor is regrettable, however, for the indigence of the ideal self may be instructive and express its function, which is to call us to the creation of ourselves by ourselves. Insofar as it is empty and indeterminate, we can freely affirm our personal uniqueness. And, owing to the infinite variety with which we can fill it at each moment, we can universalize our singularity and find in it the means of elevating nature in us, establishing the human continuity of the *thou* and the *I,* and attaining to God Himself, without the plurality of conscious selves and moments of self-awareness being annihilated by absolute unification.

THE IDEAL SELF AS INSTRUMENT OF
PERSONAL SINGULARIZATION

Classical philosophy teaches that our conduct is dominated by the search for the good and that we can withdraw from good only by moving backwards. But the ethics that philosophers have tried to build on this remark has usually been spoiled either by a eudaemonism that grossly ignores the extremities of moral option and the complexities of psychological motivation, or, on the contrary, by a formalism so empty of any content that the interest and meaning of the initial observation on which it rests can no longer be seen.

The true scope of man's quest for universal good might be better understood if it were explained that it always involves at least one determination: the search for an ideal self. *Sub specie bonitatis* is really *sub specie bonitatis meae.* This addition, which marks the passage from idea to person, certainly does not preclude our ending at an empty person after starting from an empty idea. But the emptiness that always characterizes the ideal self in certain respects is full of meaning: it separates us from ourselves to make us sensitive to the appeal of a creativity that both assures the indetermined career of our freedom and already stamps our unique imprint on all the acts our freedom will originate. In this fruitful distance between our two selves it is not the myth of Tantalus that is realized but the liberation of our spirit and the experience of our uniqueness.

The appearance of the ideal self is the sign that I have been delivered from natural servitude. For it inevitably implies the notion of a gift of the *I* to myself that the exterior world cannot confer on me with the forces at its disposal. The flow of cosmic events, the renewed offering of sensible qualities cannot replace the act of subjectivity; this act is expressed in the ideality of the self, i.e., in the distance between myself and nature whereby each of my actions prepares the field of another action. Were I to place my ideal in the effort to identify with nature, were I to try to annihilate my being as much as I could, the success of my plan would be, despite appearances, neither a servitude nor a pure and simple effacement of myself, since I would have become such as I would have willed myself to be. The original indetermination of my ideal expresses simultaneously the insufficiency of the determinism of things in my being and the necessity I am under of determining my being by my choice.

The appearance of the ideal self is the sign that I am free before the value of my person. I am certainly not free to deny my being in my act or, in other words, to renounce my act in my action. What is unique in me, though it be still only a hope, is imposed on me in the very will by which, in willing anything at all, I will myself, and I must ratify my will in my will. I am given a theme that I am not free to change, for it is my person, it is my freedom itself. But I am free to make variations on the theme, good or bad, and these constitute the history of my life. I can will my perdition, my annihilation, my perversion. The ideal self is sufficiently undetermined to allow me to pursue the values or the counter-values I wish, and it is sufficiently determined to keep me within the limits of myself. Strictly speaking, it would be necessary to distinguish the ideal self, which is a process or a framework, from the value-self, which is a possible content of the ideal self, but not necessarily attached to it.[1]

The appearance of the ideal self is the sign that I am delivered from all final servitude as regards a determined thou, even if it be God. With this proposition we can measure the strange negligence of certain ethical systems inspired by Aristotle which have used the universality of the good to chain us to God to the point of reducing freedom's domain, if not stifling its principle; whereas that same formal universality should have showed the immense autonomy left to each human person, if not in his origin, at least in the organization of his fidelity. With respect to others, indifference, revolt, and friendship are equally possible; this is all the more so when the other is of a higher order and his transcendence divine.

Every ideal hollows out an inner recess in the consciousness. The formation of the ideal *I* is thus the advent of a personal withinness. That is why the ideal of the self is a secret that can never be directly entrusted to sensible nature. But the ambivalence of the ideal self is found in the secret and the refusal to reveal itself. For this refusal bears two very different meanings, depending on the case. At one time I can resist for the sake of resisting through a will to exclude all others and be myself against everyone or withdrawn from everyone. At another time I can resist in order the better to give myself, and the modesty that impels me to hide my ideal withinness is nothing other than the desire to reserve myself for another whom I shall have chosen. The secret is then only the order of love, and the more a soul recollects herself far from banal communications, the more she prepares herself, perhaps, in the deepening of herself, for the encounter with God. The ideal self can thus become the instrument of a Promethean stubbornness as well as of a mystic openness.

But whatever its use, it is not to be imagined that the initial emptiness of the ideal self, while delivering us from final bondage, ever makes us capable of ontological isolation. If the self wishes to establish itself philosophically in solitude, it can do so only by dint of a reflection that first finds other centers of subjectivity facing its own and then seeks to absorb or eliminate them. Solipsism itself is thus replete with discussions on the essence and existence of the other: it comes off no better in this respect than "altruistic" philosophies. The freedom expressed by the ideal self is not the liberty to be an atom or an *I* without a *thou;* it is the freedom to mold the form and content of the relationship that binds the *I* to the *thou.* It demands a kind of solidarity appropriate to free beings and in accord with interpersonal causality.

This final statement leads us to understand that if the form of the ideal self frees and singularizes us owing to its very emptiness, it never remains completely empty but becomes the means of universalizing singularity without destroying it.

THE IDEAL SELF AS MEANS OF UNIVERSALIZING PERSONAL SINGULARITY

A constant and inevitable uneasiness drives me from the passing moment into the approaching one and casts me into the acceptance of my own change, whether it be to rediscover a high point of my past in the future or repeat there a consent I do not want to dwindle away. In this passage, the undetermined ideal of myself is determined. How and in what sense does this determination give me a universe?

The ideal self allows nature to be assimilated in the person. Indeed, once this self appears there is no longer any pure nature that can account for my development; vital psychic force has given place to a personal self, for I have chosen to express myself in qualities of nature, and by integrating them into my destiny, I transform them. Even the ideality of the self is a mixture of qualities wrested from things and intentions issuing from myself. And each time I try to grasp this self that constitutes me, whether it be under its positive or its ideal aspect, what I find concretely is only a hybrid reality, a product in which I discern a quality that can no longer be entirely natural and a singularity that cannot be perfectly disincarnate. Character is the product of this violently unified duality; child of two worlds yoked together in an embrace, it reacts on its parents. The ideal self is a part of character, and that is why it transforms the nature it expresses while realizing the person it announces.

The ideal self allows the coincidence of the I and thou in human reciprocity. For persons subject to natural exteriority, the osmosis of the *I* and *thou*—or their introception, to use W. Stern's expression—supposes the mediation of an ideal. Even then it presents many degrees and appreciable nuances.

In the first place, the ideal self may be composed of traits borrowed from others, either as a consequence of an unconscious or contagious imitation, or as a consequence of an intentional theft. In this case, of course, admiration is not benevolence. And when the jay decks himself out in the peacock's feathers he is not particularly concerned about the peacock; he is more interested in the victim's feathers than in the victim, and the latter is for him merely a means for self-decoration. Psychic borrowing scarcely impoverishes its victim, but it is usually accompanied by a perfect indifference on the part of the borrower toward the person he swindles.

Introception goes deeper when the self assumes responsibility for the goals of the other or the values he serves. Cooperation is of this type, as is also the relief of men devoted to a common cause. Moral or not, the purpose of the other becomes my purpose, I incorporate it into my own plans; in other words, I extend my horizon to include him. Thus it is that persons are associated with or follow one another in the history of communities, and communities enter into persons.

But there is no true introception when the subjects hold in common an object exterior to themselves; it is perfect only if each takes the other as the purpose of his being and makes the *I* and *thou* coincide in the chosen ideal so that each is transformed by the other. This attitude aims at bringing about a reciprocal creation. And the reciprocal creation is the most profound form of continuity possible between human persons. There the ideal *I* and the ideal *thou* are indiscernible; they rise together and exist only in the meeting of two subjects whose interaction they manifest. The fact that the renewal of the other is my own renewal, and that both exist in the same image, is a guarantee that neither the ideal *I* can consist of an illusion about the positive *I,* nor the ideal *thou* of an illusion about the positive *thou.* Indeed, the reality of virtual souls and their communion is in a way a self-sufficient act; it is not a representation in a strict sense, but a creation. Now a creation is neither an error nor a truth; it is a reality.

We have just surveyed the main stages in a personal interiorization in which the ideal *I* integrates the *thou* and is identified with it; and we have described this process as a mutual endosmosis. Apparently we have gone from egoism to love. But we must not be too hasty in concluding that reciprocity is always loving. Up to a certain point the coincidence of the *I* and *thou* can be accomplished in hatred; in any case, it can be realized in a perverse complicity, as, for example, the common will to physical suicide or moral disintegration. Side by side with the ideal couple, reciprocity admits of a diabolical couple. We cannot repeat it too often: introception is a process that lends itself indifferently to values and to countervalues. Increasing the number of participants changes nothing in the case. Hegesias Peisithanatos set his ideal on persuading all men to destroy themselves; he thought very much of others and idealized them in his own way. But the ecstasy of this collective delirium, had he achieved it, would not have been moral for being so widely shared; it would have been a psychic cancer of humanity, a communion for ruin, a love in death.

However, in contrast with this specious universality that turns against the universe, relationship between the *I* and *thou* can take on a veritable universality that is inaccessible to immoral introceptions. Certainly the domination of all minds by one mind remains a diabolic ideal, even if it is accompanied by the project of making all these minds active. But it becomes divine if the activity that one mind wishes to stir in all the others is to make them mutually universalizing and unique. At that moment omnipotence is changed into mercy, and the power of one becomes the power of all in the liberation of each. Creativity that withdraws from this universal love is less creative than if it accepted it, for it deprives itself of creation in the other. The unification of the self, the fruitfulness of action, and the universality of love are thus in mutual dependence and confer on each other their respective perfection.

The ideal I expresses the divine thou in the created person. At first it seems difficult to perceive God in the ideal self. On the one hand is not the ideal self the veil that permits us to conceal God, if there is a God, and flout Him insolently while "cultivating our garden," like Voltaire's "Candide"? On the other hand, does not the ideal self finally reduce itself to a pure ideal? At the end of the movement by which it constitutes itself does it not fade away in an absolute that suppresses it and in which there is room for neither a human *I* nor a supreme *thou?*

These general objections do not hold. The fact of introception has shown us that the ideal self is not like an impenetrable wall but rather like a kind of osmotic membrane; or, to put it more exactly, the ideal self can be the will of the *thou* in me and can be so in the two senses of the term: i.e., insofar as I will the *thou* and insofar as the *thou* wills me in a reciprocity in which the discovery and growth of two persons is now but a single act. What is noted on the human level suffices to disprove the hypothesis according to which the presence of a divine *thou* would be impossible *a priori* in the concrete intimations of the ideal self.

As for the second difficulty, relative to the dissolution of the *I* in the absolute, it has no more weight than the preceding one, for the growth of the spirit does not diminish the originality of the person: the example of the genius is there to prove that the universal vocation of the *I* does not destroy it, on the contrary it makes it ever more brilliant in all its works.

We must limit our examination to facts and ask whether the presence of the divine *thou* is necessary to account for the form or secret content the ideal self offers us. The response must be in the affirmative. Without going into a problem that lies beyond the scope of this chapter, let us at least give the following reasons:

a) I am always predisposed as to the essential characteristic of my personal being. Human consciousness, as we said above, is like a musical theme; this theme, this caused initiative that reunites us to a creator of persons, is found in the variations my ideal self composes at each moment.

b) The possibility of the limitless development of my ideal self in the realm of value is a spiritual experience independent of human encounters and not to be explained by them. This perfection to which my ideal self testifies is a vestige of God. It is all the more so if one thinks of the infinite introception the ideal self is capable of receiving in religious contemplation and prayer. It is capable of a divine measure in which the infinite of a consciousness, far from being opposed to the consciousness of the infinite, develops more and more in the acknowledgement of a transcendent being.

c) The coincidence of the ideal *I* and the ideal *thou* gives us the certitude of the presence of another; but this is only a qualitative presence and the continuation of a being that we cannot have created radically; for we only create qualities in and around ourselves. Without the recognition of a divine *thou* who raises up the being of persons, we would have no guarantee whatever of the radical presence of the other and the absolute continuity of the personal universe.

It remains to be proved that the divine *thou* active in us is not in reality a demiurgic or demoniac *thou*. Could not a God who would hate us or use us for purely esthetic ends, suggest to us the ideal development of ourself that is the motive of our existence? Would not the creation of personality be to take pleasure in absurdity and cruelty if personality is a lack of being? Yes, certainly, we reply, if personality is a negation and if it is singular only in the manner that each color is something less than white light. But the answer becomes quite different if the person is able, by knowledge and love, to equal the universe without being lost. The spirit has been compared to a transparent bubble that could expand indefinitely to the extremities of the universe. This is, as a matter of fact, its privilege, and it is a personal privilege. It never bursts or dissolves in this expansion, all it sacrifices are accidental limits and opacity. Its conversion strengthens its subjectivity, and this is where the comparison must be corrected: in the destiny of persons, increasing transparence is no longer, as it were, incompatible with individual color. Fullness of being is then the symphony of beings, although the source of being is the unity that creates and sustains them.[2]

NOTES

1. The value-self is not to be confused with the value of the self. The latter is an initial appeal that subsists throughout all the aspects of the self, including the ideal self; but the value-self is the result conformable to this appeal, the result constantly hoped for in the case of the good action and constantly frustrated in the case of the degrading one.

In short, ideality can be understood in three quite different senses: as a transcendent source, as a function, or as an accomplishment.

2. Henry Duméry, in his remarkable thesis, *Philosophie de la religion* (Paris, 1957), proposes the term "law-act" for what I prefer to call "person." No matter which word is used, the link joining spontaneity and reflection, individuality and totality, must be recognized in us, as well as the final instability of subjective development.

As for the deviations of the ideal self, Freud violently criticized them. I say nothing of this in the preceding pages, not because these criticisms are negligible, but because the ideal self is a larger and more fundamental reality than the super-ego of psychoanalysis.

6 ✦ Is Freedom Communicated?

To be free is to break away from one's causes, to take hold of one's own destiny, to become a creator of oneself. It seems, therefore, that freedom is an active isolation and, as such, contrary to communication. Does not its movement aim at constituting an empire within the empire of the universe and making personal determination possible only by refusing any heritage? Freedom is non-conformist; it reforms whatever tends to grow dull or to constitute a world other than the one carved by the fine point of our initiative. Its purity demands, on the one hand, that we ceaselessly try to escape from nature and, on the other, that we ceaselessly become our own cause and effect.

Even if a person believed he could reduce freedom to a choice between two alternatives, the simple fact of restricting the horizon of possibilities to a duality of specific directions (freedom of specification), or even to a simple uncertitude between acting and not acting in a determined direction (freedom of contradiction), would suffice to prove that liberty detaches itself as much as possible from real data in

115

order to become master of its own fate and creator of its own values. In free will the partisans of freedom have, in a word, been searching for an autonomy, a *Vollendung* in the *Entscheidung*. This autonomy, often confused with a radical independence, is evidently essential to the thinkers who insist more on self-invention than on choice.

In these conditions it seems unreasonable to hold that freedom can be communicated from one being to another. It asserts itself only in the separation of one being from all the others.

However, the thesis we have just considered is basically incomplete or false. Freedom is not simply a formal maneuver of retreat. Though it withdraws from reality, it is also a reality. It may be, as they say, a will to annihilation, but it is not an annihilation of the will; it is the fulfillment of a concrete person. Thus each freedom is distinguished from every other by an irreplaceable sign. To be free and to be oneself is one and the same thing; neither of these words contradicts the other, and that is why it is impossible to elude freedom's positive being, a fact that leads to the problem of its origin outside the subject in which it asserts itself. Liberty does not simply transcend the world, it is also transcended by it, and when it relies on itself nothing proves that it does not still depend on the world. It does not escape communication.

What is more, when considering what causes freedom to appear and positively constitutes it, we will always have to reckon with nature from which it turns away. No matter how spontaneous freedom may appear, it needs an isthmus to connect it with matter and society, the experience of the past, and the spectacle of space. There is no free act that is not a liberation and no liberation that is not owing to a challenge. Freedom is always bound by the circumstances that bring it into being, or, what amounts to the same thing, the tyrants that threaten it. I am not my own cause or creator except as a consequence of external stimuli. Whether it be a question of the need to earn a living or any other circumstantial cause of my prompt reaction, I am myself only at the center of what is not myself and in response to the challenge I find therein.

But must we not recognize that in a certain manner all things communicate freedom to us? Or if that statement is too bold, let us at least admit that a kind of complicity of all beings is the preliminary condition of the autonomy that some of them can give one another. This complicity proceeds not only from the gentle invitation by which nature suggests that we lift ourselves above it, but also from the ultimatum it proposes and the tragedies into which it lures us. There is a pre-established harmony, even though there is also a bitter experience, in the fact that extreme goods (in this case, the affirmation of self) are often born of extreme evils.

The fact that we have alluded to circumstantial causes in this context should suffice to show that we do not deny the discontinuity subsisting between the appeal of nature and the response of the person. The world lends itself to the liberation of man, it does not engender it. One can give only what one has, and freedom does not receive its being from what it leaves, but finds there the target or the stepping stone whereby it develops itself.

We can now examine the case in which the freedom of the self does not originate in a non-self but is produced in the radiance of another self by whom it is willed. The education of a child and the vocation of a disciple provide special examples of this. Does the will to awaken freedom in others really depend on the parents or teachers? It would be hard to deny this, if they are worthy of their mission. But that will is praiseworthy and ultimately more real only in proportion as it is associated with more intelligence and disinterestedness. Great souls often radiate their influence without thinking of it; they do not try to exercise influence with a persistence that bewitches or stifles. The sincere intention of freeing another self is neither exasperated nor exasperating.

Now, is this will efficacious? And precisely in what could a liberating influence consist? One answer might be to deny all transitive causality and see in this liberation nothing but the suppression of certain obstacles. To teach a child to be itself is not to act directly on the center of its being, for this eludes us, but on the periphery of the dispositions and habits that surround the germ of personality. All we can do, in short, is turn over to the child a system of expression conformed to the demands of a given civilization; or, to adopt the more generous formula used above, we teach him what favors the growth of his autonomy, on the supposition that the young person already bears the germ of it in himself.

There is something quite proper in this modesty. We can never really create another's personality or liberty whole and entire. Even the most docile baby will develop into an unpredictable being, to the surprise of the parents who know neither whence he came nor whither he is going. However, though interpersonal influence is not total, it does constitute a fact so decisive and disturbing that we cannot liken it to a simple removal of external obstacles. When we examine our past we know very well that our initiatives proceed from personal contacts that did not act on us from without but by a strange intussusception. Therefore we must try to push our analysis farther.

There are several phases in the experience of the communication of freedoms.

1) First of all, the mother-freedom imposes on the daughter-freedom a perspective that causes it to be by and for itself. This moment is very mysterious, but it is in the very texture of interpersonal relations. The act by which I choose myself at the very outset is at the same time the act by which I discover that "I am launched" in being. This initial act, which is also an acceptance and a position, still subsists in the absence of all intervention of the other and is probably explained only by a divine causality of our selfhood. But we discover it again on another plane and in a lesser degree at the heart of our dealings with men. My encounter with a radiant, free being is already my liberation and my own freedom; to perceive it is to be what it wants me to be; I am at once by it and by myself, not in imitating it as an exterior model (which would be the mere contagion of example), but in awakening to myself within the perspective of our encounter; there the gift it offers me and the position I take are identical.

Since this act is free, it is not surprising that its form should be so too; aside from the received intimacy or caused initiative that impresses its mark on it, nothing in it is foreseeable. To awaken to freedom under the influence of another is neither necessarily to think of self nor to think of the other but to acquire a mode of life that is immediately expressed in the objects or sentiments one has chosen. It is often by a slow spiritual deepening that a consciousness thus engendered learns to identify accurately the particular sources of its being and freedom. If a rule could be deduced in this respect, it would no doubt be that the offspring is at first ungrateful. This ingratitude flows necessarily from the authoritarian character of the earliest influences: the very depth of the imprint received seems compensated by a restoration of the look, and the burden of the past disappears before the promise of the future. The awakening freedom is indebted for its being, yet it seems to be an absolute beginning, a *tabula rasa.*

Ultimately we should dissociate the necessary or certain character of the influence from the foreseeable character of the acts that the influenced freedom will posit. Only one thing is predictable: the theme that has been induced; the variations are not.

2) But the theme must include variations; and this leads us to a new moment in freedom. We propose to call it *derived freedom,* in contrast with the original freedom we have just discussed. If the first act of freedom is to ratify its being and will it necessarily, the second is to call it in question and be able to deny it up to a certain point. The form of autonomy that is properly ours includes the capacity to alienate it, in a measure, and to repudiate our ancestors, or use them as a freedom that no longer wants to be free.

It is this element of negation and possible revolt that is most often retained in the definition of freedom. In the *De libero arbitrio,* St. Augustine judges that defective freedom alone is properly ours: sin is from us alone and not grace, that is, the divine liberality diffused in us. He thus brought into sharp relief an idea already familiar to the Greeks, and modern thinkers have concluded from it that the only thing that is truly ours and truly free is the recessive, if not absolutely Luciferian, freedom whose claims we mentioned at the beginning of this study. But St. Augustine, for all the ardor of his anti-Pelagian polemic, had not really isolated derived freedom from the totality of the divine plan. Good and bad variations are still relative to a primitive theme; the will that isolates itself does so only in its vocation to totality, and this overflows its retreat on all sides.

Moreover, this phase of possible negation is conformed to the wish of every paternal generosity that asserts itself in order to propose, rather than impose, itself. To educate a free being is to affect it in such a way that it can leave us. Since such is the creative will, the rebellion of the progeny may be the creator's worry but not his defeat, for he has assumed the risk of opposition.

3) While the theme supposes the necessity of variations and outlives their eventual mediocrity, it must also be added that the variations are subject to an immanent law of progress which will also be eventually a law of correction and conversion. The discovery of this norm at the heart of caprice and anarchy is the third and last term in the dialectic of freedom. Planted deep within the act, it binds the act to that from which it madly wanted to free itself in order to be the principle of its real emancipation.

Clinging to liberty like the tunic of Nessus, the value of my liberty that I recognize or freely ignore but do not create, is the very communication of my purest freedom. This it is that reveals the *raison d'être* of the two preceding phases; the autonomy of the theme and the autonomy of the variations are joined in the autonomy of a value that conquers its very datum, since we find the rule of our progress in the test of emancipation. Nothing could unite solitude and solidarity more closely. Freedom is thus called to recreate the grace it had received and reopen the communication it may have thought it had cut off. The continuity of persons, which at first seemed assured by the perception of influence, now gives place to a continuity that is much more interior, in which the very bond that we have received is born of our reflection. The Other was designating me by giving me to myself; henceforth I designate the Other by seeking myself in me.

Let us add that for the vague "antecedent *we*" of the initial phase, we can henceforth substitute the "consequent *we*" of associated free beings. The image that is their common work expresses the convergence of their enterprises.

Thus one can glimpse the possible solution of the two principal antinomies of the communication of freedom:

a) Freedom both triumphs and fails when it engenders another freedom. It seems contradictory that it should be fulfilled in restraint and exposed to annihilation by the independence or aggression of its offspring. To this tragic difficulty we can answer that the creative will is invulnerable in its very essence, not only because it assumes the risk and the negation of the other, but even more so because it is realized in the other in a much more complex process than either risk or negation.

b) Some will say, however, that a received freedom is no longer free. To which we reply that the efficacy of a gratuitous influence does not end in the original freedom of the other; it also supposes his derived liberty and the discovery of his norm of autonomy. At no time in this development is the victory of the liberating will assured by an alleged predictability of conduct. Thus there is no question of choosing between grace and freedom or necessity and contingence in a domain where each one of these notions has meaning only by reason of the reality of the others, for the communication of freedom is realized in their communion.

7 ✧ The Forms of the We

Collective consciousness is the consciousness of the *we*. But it is far from being homogeneous. It always includes at least an embryonic sense of an *I* and *thou;* however this often occurs without the deep personalization of the *I* and *thou*. Therefore we must distinguish a host of forms and degrees in collective consciousness. The following schema is a tentative classification.[1]

UNDIFFERENTIATED "WE"

This is an extremely weak consciousness that would, in the extreme, be equivalent to a kind of vegetative sense, anterior to any reflection and even to any particular representation. Neither the subject that senses it nor the *thou* it joins are discernible from the background of community solidarity. Likewise, this group is indistinguishable from other groups: its boundaries and content are equally vague. To adopt F. Perroux's expression, it is a *we* of indistinction. Undetermined though it be, it is, however, likely to have varying intensities.

124

It is all the more intense as the beings it gathers together are:

1) *Qualitatively more alike.* For example, we doubtless have the vague impression of being one with the cosmos, a landscape, or material objects; or again with the vital force that animates the plants, animals, and people around us. But the feeling is weak and unperceived in this case. On the contrary, without being more distinct, it becomes stronger when we sense it with regard to human beings and, especially, with regard to our compatriots, our family, individuals of our own generation, etc. In any crowd the consciousness that "de-partitions" individuals and welds them into one is all the more lively as these are stripped of all their differences and their psychic character is reduced to a single quality (fear, admiration, anger, etc.)

2) *Quantitatively more numerous.* Crowd psychology shows this again, and also the psychology of all kinds of mass consciousness.

3) *Closer in space and time.* This is why the common feeling of the masses is less strong than the self-awareness of a crowd. It is true that centers of attention help the masses to effect their rapprochement. This is the purpose served by posters and newspapers, for example. In the crowd itself the leader's slogans, gestures, and facial expressions are mirrors that prevent the spatial separation of the individuals. A crowd directed by a strong agitator is not strictly speaking a differentiated crowd; the presence of the demagogue is only a pseudo-differentiation; he helps the crowd be more purely a crowd, i.e., a collection of "de-cerebrated" individuals. It may happen that he is directing the crowd according to an intelligent plan, but this is beside the point. In the measure

that he participates in the common consciousness, the same current flows through him as through the others; his sole function is to be passively the lens that catches the rays of light and magnifies them to the burning point.

The intensity of the *we* does not mean that it is mentally active. Though it moves muscles it does not renew minds; it is simply a spontaneous and compelling sentiment that is born when individuality abdicates.

DIFFERENTIATED "WE'S"

Unlike the simply lived *we* just alluded to, the forms of collective consciousness we are going to consider suppose distinct representations of the whole and the parts. We will examine the situational *we,* the functional *we,* the interpersonal *we,* and the *we* of theandric relation.

The situational "we".—This is the name I give collective consciousness accompanied by a representation of the multiplicity of its members; but each individuality is simply lodged there in a portion of space and time, and its psychic originality is still scarcely considered. This is the application to the *we,* of a system of geometric, geographic, or historic indicators. The locations of the component points are established: such an element is next to such another, or in front of it, or behind it. The community and its members are seen in the spectacle and are thus passive, but our knowledge of it is objective; it is no longer the foggy sense of the undifferentiated *we.* We imagine a field of forces constituted by a gathering together of animated bodies; we are not interested in the inner life of the participants; they are mere numbers as far as we are concerned; but at least we distinguish them from each other and situate them in the whole by the determination of their place. We could still say it is a question of a localized *we*.

It is apposite, therefore, to show the distinction between masses at a distance ("we business men," "we soldiers" . . .) and masses nearby (the consciousness of pupils in a classroom, of travelers in a bus . . .) and also of aggregates or groups (passersby on the street, witnesses to an accident . . .). In contrast with a system of localized selves, collective consciousness can thence represent to itself other systems of distribution. It can class the inhabitants of a village in a number of ways (communities of men, women, farmers, craftsmen, etc.), and a single individual can be a member of an unlimited number of distinct systems to which it belongs by different titles. In any case, the *we* that I am examining disregards the nature of the roles; it is only a series of distributions. It is collective consciousness *sub specie quantitatis*. In the undifferentiated *we* these quantitative relations affected collective consciousness without its being aware of it; in the present instance the *we* grasps itself intellectually in its quantitative and especially its geographic structure.

The functional "we".—This is the most important form of objective group consciousness. Here we imagine not only positions but functions. The main ideas inherent in it can readily be enumerated as follows:

1) Individual qualities are ascribed to members of the group: each is distinguished from the others by something other than his place.

2) Each one has a role to play in the whole; he serves the group either passively or actively.

3) The group itself has its own function which results from its components but which is also expressed in them and can go beyond them. It is not a simple addition but a synthesis.

4) The group, while having its originality and specific functional character, also has a history; it evolves or can evolve.

5) The consciousness of being part of a group is accompanied by the consciousness of being able to form subgroups (for example, the relation of comradeship between two members of a team), or enlarge or enrich the *we* of the group itself (other members can be added to the group).

6) Qualities can be communicated among the members of the group or between the group and its members.

7) The group and its action can be in contact with other groups and actions situated outside the circle of the functional *we*.

8) The group is not only in contact with its members within itself and with other groups nearby but also with a value and an idea incarnated in it. Thus the idea of the family is manifested in the institutional structure revealed in history, and its value is expressed by the place it occupies in the hierarchy of social ends offered to the moral perceptions of persons.

In this kind of collective consciousness there is a whole set of very complex reciprocities. Each one knows not only that he possesses and uses the others but that he belongs to them and serves them. Moreover, it is essential to community consciousness that each one recognize the presence in the others of an intellectual awareness similar to his own. Of course, communion in the same objective representation cannot be absolute, and each sees the whole according to a perspective adjusted to that of the others more readily than it identifies itself with it perfectly. But the objective *we* supposes faith, at least in this correspondence.

The structure of the functional *we* comprises three principal elements:

An idea and a value of which the group is the vehicle or witness and which can be of a vital, psychic, spiritual, or other kind of order;

The collective feeling itself and the representations or tendencies related to it. We discern that the community to which we belong is different according as it is:

a) Qualitatively composed of a common sharing of will, memory, sentiments, etc.;

b) More or less broad or voluminous;

c) More static or more dynamic;

d) More convergent or more divided;[2]

e) More or less autonomous (really, on this plane no collective consciousness goes so far as to feel self-sufficient; the consciousness of being a citizen of the world is as threatened and dependent, if not more so, than that of being a villager; it depends on values that are not the very conscience of the group; besides, every functional group supposes the thought of other groups, be they rivals or friends);

The representation of individuals and their reciprocal functions. The inventory of these relations can be attempted in several ways; let us point out at least:

—The hostility of the members: this is the *we* of war (my adversary and myself);

—Domination by one or several members and subjection of the others (the feudal *we*);

—Egalitarian collaboration by an identical attitude on the part of each, by the complementarity of diverse functions (this is the distinction that Durkheim makes between mechanical and organic society), or by substitution and alternance (*we* playing see-saw).

It would be interesting to try to deduce some laws related to the consciousness of the functional community according as one or the other element of its structure predominates in the representation. Here, by the way of example, are some possible notations in this direction:

1) The predominance of *value* in the conscious representation will tend to erase, by definition, the group feeling and the feeling for individuals in the functional *we;* but it will accelerate the historical development of the idea in the group in which it is embodied. In this case value is comparable to the sun; and the idea it embodies in the group is comparable to the plant the sun makes grow. This growth will be accelerated because the value and the idea, instead of acting only as efficient causes, will now further act as final causes sought for themselves (e.g., the exaltation of the values of courage, work, power, etc., will hasten the development of the "national idea" in history; a country that is aroused by these goals takes on the awareness its citizens have of a new form and more quickly realizes the potentialities of its destiny).

2) The predominance of the *collective sense* itself threatens to make the *we* more egotistical, more vague (especially if this *we* is broad or voluminous: no distinct representation of its members is possible in this case, even

with good will, as can be seen in the feeling of large communities such as a city or a country; this will be all the more true when one tries systematically to separate the representation of the participants from the consciousness of the whole). But on the other hand, the exaltation of the sense of a pure community will tend to make the functional *we* more intense and durable. This is doubtless why party or patriotic propaganda does not hesitate to make use of it. The fact that the community here takes itself as its object prevents it from falling back into an undifferentiated *we* like that of the crowd which, deprived of this representation of itself, is doubtless an intense consciousness but also an unstable one.

3) The predominance of the *representation of the members* and their mutual functions in the whole, will threaten the permanence of the original *we* and easily lead to the rise of persons. The latter are always born in a social group and their destiny is to detach themselves from it in order to be faithful to their own vocation; for they do not have to be instruments or expressions of a natural society but the free agents of a spiritual realm. Directly threatened by the claim of the participants, the functional community can, however, benefit from it in certain respects; in fact, it is the consideration of individuals that obliges society to reform itself and be impregnated little by little with personal works, which is what civilization is. The functional *we* thus becomes more discerning, more careful about justice in the laws it formulates.

In short, the predominance of values in the *we* under examination ends in a *flowering of institutions;* the predominance of the pure sense of community leads to blind habits or *traditions;* the predominance of individual particularities, despite its ferments of crises or anarchy, brings about the birth of *progress,* not only because it constrains the group conscience to reform but because it permits the *we* of psychology to emerge from the *we* of sociology.

The personal "we," or "we" of love.—The personal *we* is realized only by love because with love alone is the complete communion of persons possible. What characterizes this form of communal consciousness is actually the will to promote a *thou* and be promoted by him. There follows a heterogeneous continuity of centers of consciousness and a double centrifugal possession in the other that we analyzed earlier. While everything remains subordinated to an objective task or proceeds from it in the bio-social, functional *we,* it is the development of the persons themselves that love wills; and consequently the essential aim is no longer that of the object but of the subject. Specifically, it is not the aim of a limited subject but of an *I* and a *thou* who are universal perspectives beyond all the social communities nature offers us.

That it is very difficult to live this subjective *we* without mixing a natural representation in it and degrading it into an objective *us,* has already been frankly conceded in the course of this study. Only the dyad allows a direct communion of persons; even then it is intermittent. Beyond it, the *we* almost certainly loses its personal distinctness and sinks into the larger but inferior forms enumerated in the preceding paragraphs.

The "we" of theandric relation.—This is what unites the personal consciousness to the divine Absolute; it is by a creative will of God that it can really explain its origin and the identity of its essential ideal, thanks to which it subsists and is unified independently even of its earthly encounters.

NOTES

1. For those who wish to study the problem, I recommend: G. Gurvitch, *Essais de sociologie* (Paris, 1939), pp. 9–112; W. McDougall, *The Group Mind* (Cambridge, 1920); the indispensable *Handwörterbuch der Soziologie,* edited by Vierknadt; and the fourth Semaine Internationale de Synthèse, devoted to *La Foule* (The Crowd), Paris, 1934.

2. Convergence or condensation of the group must not be bound to differentiation of the members of the group. A clan is convergent, but its members are not differentiated; a commercial enterprise has differentiated members, but can itself be more or less convergent.

III · The Limits of Communication

8 ⋄ *The Notion of Mask*

THE APPEARANCE OF THE PERSON

The term "mask" is often applied to the self as it appears to others, regardless of what it may know itself to be. This application of the word is too broad, and philosophical language would do well to avoid it. What a person is for others when he does not suspect it would better be called his *appearance*. It includes two very dissimilar aspects: on the one hand, the immediate radiance of the personality through the body and, on the other, a series of qualities that are, so to speak, pinned onto the body without expressing in the least the inmost being.

A single cast of features may show these two types of significance. For example, goodness that is readily seen in the expression of the face may be, in certain cases, a true reflection of the interior dispositions that emanate from a man without his being aware of it; in other cases, it may be deposited on his features like a natural varnish covering up indifference or meanness. Appearance is equivocal, and that is why it is imprudent to judge people by their expression.

The intuition had of the other is never instantaneously pure, or at least never instantaneously sure of its purity.

The first of these two very different allusions doubtless betrays an intention of the subject, and in that respect it could be called a mask. But that is a general intention which penetrates the body like a light shed through a diffusing lens without being directed toward any particular object. Thus the joy that emanates from a young and pure person reveals his inmost being to the eyes of all, even though it was meant for no spectator in particular. It is a fact that a human person, even in sleep, always allows something of himself to be seen; he is cast into this world, he is turned toward it by an inevitable and primitive movement of his will. Thus any consent to live implies a minimum of love for the encounters one will have as a consequence. But the love this person has for the beings of the world to whom he is offered is global; he loves none of them specially; he does not yet know their precise individuality; he is perceived by them without having drawn their attention to himself and without understanding the gaze they turn on him. Furthermore, and above all, he first surrenders himself ingenuously without trying to use his radiance to heighten his effects. He does not become an instrument for himself in his exterior action. That is why appearance, under this form, is not properly speaking a "mask."

We often disregard the vital or psychic expressions shown on the face or in behavior that does not truly reflect a disposition of the self, and yet it is to these that almost all the misconceptions we have of others are due. Very frequently appearance is not only irrelevant to the self but contrary to it. Neither the observers nor the subject know this at first. An expression full of sweetness may hide a hardened soul; a nonchalant curve of the arm may conceal a will of steel. . . . But as long as the self is not concerned about its appearance it cannot make a mask of it, and it is really only a *semblance,* not only in the sense of something that rises in front of the observer but also in the sense of something that misleads perception and launches it on a false trail.

The difficulty of distinguishing true expression from pseudo-expression is real, but not insuperable. Each time a subject is attentive, he reveals himself. His manner of eating, working, and suffering, allows the deep lines of his insertion into life to show through; his timidity or his ambition, his emotivity, his introverted or extroverted character. . . . Methodical observation permits one to read rather quickly the basic intentions and directions they follow; furthermore, it provides an insight into the unique originality that is personality itself. But the basic problem is to know when the real intentions stop and when to avoid adding pseudo-intentions to them. The movement of the hand is really felt under the glove, but the glove is added to the substance of the hand. While recognizing certain authentic aspects of the other, we always run the risk of ascribing to him traits that he does not have, or that he is simply wearing like clothes. Love's disillusionment often results from the lover's not perceiving the character traits of the beloved that would make it very difficult to work in common with him. But more often he has really remarked their presence, only he thought they were compensated for, or negated by, other aspects he mistakenly thought were just as deep, whereas they did not emanate from the actual person. This mistake can be made without there having been the least pretense on the part of the loved one. Are we not all, especially in youth, clothed with qualities we have not yet integrated and do not even know we are wearing?

Whatever the simple emanation of the self may be, or the qualities pinned onto it, appearances do evolve. They succeed each other like images on a screen. The novelist who has most pitilessly analyzed this succession and was most sensitive to its discontinuity, is Marcel Proust. In the second part of *Le Temps Retrouvé* (*The Past Recaptured*) he describes the ravages of time on the human being. After a twenty year absence he finds it impossible to recognize most of the persons he knew. Some of them appear "to extend still further the limits which the transformation of the human body can attain."[1] It is a mutation reminiscent of a too-perfect disguise; "Those strange faces they have been developing unintentionally for a long time cannot be removed with a little soap and water" (p. 256). Others change much less in the zoological order than in the order of character, or at least the two changes combine: "The lean, scrawny young girl had become a portly, indulgent dowager. One might say that in a social and moral sense it was a different person" (p. 259). In all cases of this kind, the new appearance crowds out and takes the place of the preceding ones, and this is what seems to have most caught the novelist's attention.

But the evolution of appearance can be quite different; it can *recapitulate* in the present a long voyage in the past. Rembrandt's portraits are excellent examples of this; his subjects wear their history on their faces. In a painting like the "Prodigal Son," the diversity of the roads followed by the father, the repentant son, and the elder son is admirably shown on the canvas. It is hardly necessary to know the Gospel parable in order to comment on the scene and discover the narrative.

Finally, there are appearances that are *prophetic*. They announce in the infant the toothless grin of the old man. It is a cruel and, alas, a rather simple sport to guess on which side the edifice will lean and fall; it has its weak points, and its future is already exposed to the prophetic vision of a discerning observer.

THE EXTERIOR MASK

The exterior mask is constituted when the self becomes aware of having an appearance in the eyes of others. This representation of the self for others modifies one's behavior and enables him to act on others through the image they have of him.

We already meet this phenomenon in the animal kingdom where we can observe masquerades and calculated acts. The spider and the praying mantis use a mask of insensibility to surprise their victims, and at the same time they turn away, by their strange or terrible character, creatures stronger than themselves whose prey they might have become; they simulate a power of attack they do not possess. The *prochile lippu* wears a seductive mask: it moves its victims to pity (man included) by crying like a child in distress; then it leaps on the unwary one who approaches, and sucks his blood. The young of mammals try to attract their parents' or wardens' attention and solicitude by a kind of play-acting which would seem to be something more than a series of reflexes. Müller-Freienfels gives some curious examples of associational masks: certain visitors to ant hills gain admittance by exploiting their resemblance to their ant hosts (*Psychologie des Alltags,* p. 251). So long as role-playing is conscious, it belongs to the processes of adaptation. In general, harmless and weak animals go beyond the reflex zone in this activity; they are the ones who must resort to subtle and refined simulation for self-protection. Unable to defend themselves by a purely bodily mechanism, they achieve their purpose by representing to themselves the effect that their changed appearance will have on the spectators; consequently they pretend. Very probably the beginnings of reflection and the aptitude for adopting the point of view of another have their biological roots in beings that are muscularly inferior and obliged, like Ulysses, to use wile to overcome the powerful ones of this world. We should certainly not be too quick to ascribe our ways of acting to animals, even domestic ones; but it is incontestable that many vertebrates are capable of looking at themselves in others' eyes and experiencing a being-for-others.

With man, this procedure occupies an enormous place and dominates all interpsychology. We know we are visible, audible, palpable; we experience how others change their attitude toward us when our features are spontaneously modified, or when we change the rhythm and manner of our movements. Hence we subject our gestures and expression of emotion to a masked action. The image of ourselves in the other is doubtless not perceived exactly as in a mirror: if I am angry I do not see the flush on my cheeks nor the fire in my eyes, but I can feel my blood boil and know that the other detects a correlative alteration in my appearance.

So it is from within that I know my dumb-show, and it is the inner face of my exterior mask that I direct, regulating myself simultaneously by the reactions of the other and the variations in my game. Something escapes me in the interval: the direct view of my own being from outside. That is why some masked behavior is awkward, why some grimaces do not have the desired effect, or miss the mark and fall in a void. Coquettish old ladies do not see how ridiculous they are because the defects in their faces always outnumber their artifices and exceed their imagination, even when they are advised by a mirror, or beauticians, or friends.

This inaptitude of the self to know its whole bodily appearance and set itself squarely in the line of vision of the other proves that the reciprocity of minds is not absolute in our masquerade nor can wills completely communicate in it. But there is nevertheless a correlation of masks, in the sense that I act on the other by my mask in the measure that the other, too, has an appearance, and that I perceive his mask. The body thus obliges each person to go partly outside himself and become alternately the hunter and the game. In this adventure, the self loses and regains, by turns, the presence of the other in itself and its own presence in that of the other.

But not all masks are corporeal. Man has created symbols of himself that are, as it were, extensions of his body and complicate his mask. The most remarkable of these is clothing. He has also invented that prodigiously subtle kind of mask which is language. Whereas natural expression remains attached to the body and finally dissolves there like waves in the sea, clothes and language are detached from us. Artificial symbols, being separable, can also be moved about. We are not condemned to be always presenting them to others, as is the case with our nose or mouth; these symbols form a changeable décor.[2] They relieve the mental strain of always trying to correct our face to serve our intentions. Thanks to them, we do not have to resign ourselves to having a certain kind of face and sacrifice our intentions to it when the conflict becomes unbearable—like the man who having a naturally stupid look and not succeeding in changing it, decides to act stupid and makes a virtue of necessity.

Artificial masks are, in a word, very convenient. They are more readily available than the others; and at the same time they are farther removed from us. They thus accentuate the paradox inherent in the bodily mask. The latter brings my appearance close to my reality, since it supposes that I am aware of my being in the eyes of the other and choose one of the aspects of my appearance to express myself to him. On the other hand, the bodily mask removes my appearance from myself, for it is exterior; I only express myself through it in order to disguise myself. Even if I sincerely want to translate my meaning in a smile, by the fact that I use it as a thing, I make that smile something that I distinguish from my inmost being; for an agent cannot be identical with the instrument he uses.

There is an ambiguity in all the aspects under which I want to act on the other by varying the image he has of me. The role of the exterior mask is multiple: it can make the self impenetrable or, on the contrary, it can expedite the communication of a state of soul or an intention I want to convey to another.[3] At one time I simply hide behind my mask, at another I disguise myself and present myself as someone other than I am; at still another I transform my appearance and make it reveal my being more faithfully.

The two essential functions of the exterior mask are, in brief, to disguise the self and by this means form the attitude of the *thou* toward it. But the goal cannot be perfectly attained; the action that tends toward it soon turns against itself. And this failure in calculation, far from surprising us, ought to prove to us that the fundamental *I-thou* relationship is not a mathematically calculated thing; being spiritual, it cannot be entirely transposed in terms of nature.

We grant that the mask is supposed to hide the self. But who will deny that it reveals it, too? It has often been remarked that masked balls shed light on the hidden dispositions or repressed tendencies of each guest. And in the theater world not every actor is made for every role. It is the same way with life. If I like to put on airs, I betray my taste for show and a life of ease; if I decide to keep still, I reveal my taciturn character. If I think only of humiliating myself, I show my pride; and if I change my mask with each of my interlocutors, I publicly declare that I am given to role-playing.

On the other hand, the exterior disguise is meant to modify the other's attitude. But the gambler is caught in his trick. To want to change others is to change oneself. To assume a role is to be captured by the role. We end by becoming what we meant only to appear to be. Function creates the man; in a large measure the *personnage* makes the person. A fearful mother eventually acquires courage by reassuring her child; a surly person becomes amiable by practicing business diplomacy. No doubt the role does not completely absorb the individual; but it takes a minimum of aptitude to play a role, and eventually we are transformed by the pretense we adopt.[4] It is still ourselves we are obeying while we enjoy the fruit of our adaptation to the social milieu. To sum up, the exterior mask can neither isolate me without betraying me, nor turn me toward society without drawing it toward myself.

THE INTERIOR MASK

For every exterior mask there is invariably an interior one, that is, the self-image that I offer to myself. I imagine what I am so that I can act on myself and become other than I was. The elements of this private *personnage* are often borrowed from the appearance of others. A child dreams of being a sailor because he has seen some sailors; he then imagines he is one and splits his personality so he can look at himself. He stands back and gives himself a fictitious form under which he contemplates himself. However, others give him only the material for his mask, and it is not absolutely necessary that he try to grasp his bodily appearance by placing himself as it were outside his body.

The pure form of the interior mask is quite different: it is an intramural game in which the splitting of the personality can be effected with mental data alone and does not set itself up in space. For example, I give myself a mask of justice and honorableness composed of sentiments relative to myself and having no need of sensible data exhibited in space. It is mainly in time that I dialog with myself and feel my multiplicity. I find within myself the thousand aspects of my past; some of these have been repeated; they bear on my present like habits; they are the personnages to whom I am subject. Thus the inferiority complex is composed of depressing, and often too precise, memories of my former ways of acting.

Then there are the personnages of the future: I anticipate the decision I am going to make, by clearly representing to myself the kind of person I want to become. My expression is then one of self-invention and constitutes the program of my activity. Sometimes I build my future with my past; I renew relations with an aspect of myself that I had been neglecting. In many moral crises, for example, I try to match myself with a precious moment I once lived in the past, but with which I had lost contact, and that now appears to me as half foreign. Therefore, I bring it back before my eyes like a fugitive that has just been caught. As a matter of fact, in the mask there is always a memory of my past and an anticipation of my future united in my present representation. The only variant is the quantity of old and new elements.

Every interior mask is located between the two extremes of pure intimacy and absolute strangeness. It is a half-self that I have not yet absorbed or have ceased to enclose. Consequently it is always at a certain moral distance from the innermost *I*. And there are many degrees in the tension by which I bind it to my act. There are masks that I put on to amuse myself without ever seriously intending to assimilate them; for example, there are sallies into daydreaming. They serve me as an alibi. Thanks to them I console my everyday self and put on my "Sunday best." Sometimes it is impossible to achieve the reality of the mask; it may be too Utopian: the shepherdess imagines she is a queen. Then again it may be possible without being probable: the queen would like to become a shepherdess. There are other masks we are not content merely to hold before us; they descend into our very substance, but cannot take over our whole being; they involve us in their rivalries and agonizing discords; we feel two men within ourselves. Finally, there are some that are like a happy and stimulating echo of the regular rhythm of our growth; they support and amplify our personal fulfillment in the progressive unity of our selves.

The more closely the mask is associated with our interior life, the more durable it tends to be; but also the more it tends to suppress the distance between it and our selves, and consequently to suppress itself as a mask. If it continues to maintain itself on the periphery, it hides us from ourselves more than it transforms us. But while we escape in a fantastic dream, we still unfortunately change ourselves; we foster our paralysis and convert it into an impossible repose. We try to stop within ourselves the vital impulse of our being. Megalomania is only an extreme example of this attitude that wrenches us from our true self and plunges us into a stubborn, sterile madness.

We change the aspect of our possibilities in the succeeding moments of our existence, so that masks are rivals seeking to dominate and dislodge one another from the first place. The same individual may thus be a swashbuckler today and a coward tomorrow; he may be a poet at dawn and turn prosaic when evening comes. But there is not one of these images that impresses itself at a given moment without the others being outlined in the shadows; they form his distinctive entourage like the swaying, shadowy crowd surrounding the idol of a day, or like the harmonics that give the distinctive timbre to a fundamental note. Thus the multiplicity stirring within us is not only historically successive but also simultaneous in time; beneath the conscious faces there is the immense range of faces that are not conscious, or only partially so. They often develop at the expense of compromises and the invention of a new disguise that masks the mask itself or divides it into various aspects; we do not always frankly accept the image we want the most and the role we hope to be assigned; we cleverly alter it, and it changes its form to please us by anticipating our desires, so to speak. Freud has given a masterly analysis of this phenomenon with reference to dream symbols; the repressed tendency is transposed in order to deceive the vigilance of the Censor—but the customs officer and the smuggler are fundamentally in agreement, the one closing his eyes and the other bowing to a pseudo-control. This is because both are still our self, and our personality is never really split in the incessant fiction in which we build our reality.

In the final analysis, interior masks are the manifestation of an incomplete personality and can result from the will to fulfillment or from the effort to escape the vertigo in which personality is depersonalized. This is why interior masks follow a course between a minimum and a maximum of consciousness, without ever reaching the ultimate, which would be either the pure unconscious or absolute consciousness. These masks are formed before our eyes, but they proceed from our substance and eventually return to it. Whenever we seek their elements in the shadowy spontaneity of the vital spirit, our person mimics nature's unconscious in order to snatch them from it; thus they appear devoid of consciousness. But if they triumph afterwards in the luminous apotheosis our choice confers on them, they become our self only by disappearing within us; their success is no longer their consciousness, for they die in ours; and it was only by our complicity that they seemed to be distinguished from us. Thus they are entirely dependent on the fruitful hesitations of our becoming. What is our character but the encounter of these two movements, the one proceeding from an elemental spirit and the other from a personal intention? It introduces nature's evolving determinism into our being, and in that nature it expresses the inventive choice of our person.

MASKS AND THE I-THOU RELATION

In their mutual relations, the *I* and *thou* can form a functional or objective *we* whose principal element is the action of exterior masks. Several types suggest themselves:

1) I can try to put on a mask by trying to mask the other; I then turn away from my real partner and try to turn him away from my real self. Such, for example, is "the ostrich policy"; such also is love based on illusion, choosing a fictitious appearance of the beloved and the lover to guide its work.

2) I can try to unmask the other by putting on a mask myself; of all interpsychological relationships this is doubtless the most common. When it is adopted by the partner also, the situation easily becomes a conflict. Although it can be made to serve a partnership or a friendship, it is in combat that it is most strikingly revealed.

3) Trying to take off my own mask while masking the other to myself, may seem to be an unusual attitude, unsuitable for adaptation. It is found in all cases of naivete or foolish confidence. Nevertheless, this it is that intervenes, in certain respects, in the educative process. For the educator tries to insert his sincerest desire into a being whose secret he must respect; sometimes he must close his eyes to certain traits in his pupil, just as the sculptor has to forget the marble and think only of the statue. But this tactic would be dangerous unless it were provisory and alternated with other procedures.

4) Finally, my purpose may be to unmask both myself and the other. This is not the apanage of love alone; it is also associated with open hatreds and all the circumstances in which masks fall.

It would be still more complicated if the analysis were applied up to the subtlest divisions, and separated the mechanism of the interior mask into the relations of personalities by multiplying the four preceding situations. Thus that *I* may try to conceal or reveal itself not only with respect to the other, but also with respect to itself. Similarly, he can try to veil or unveil his partner's behavior, at one time in order to modify himself and at another in order to act on his partner. In love-as-illusion, which we have just used as an example, the Utopian representation may be intended to provoke self-intoxication or, on the contrary, to charm the other. These two ends can even be pursued simultaneously by the same subject.

Since each of these intentions may or may not be that of the other with regard to the self, the number of possible relations of the *I* and *thou* is considerable. The perception of others and the modes of interaction between persons are so varied as to make predictions impossible. But even when data concerning the actual behavior of the persons are lacking, the framework of their possible behavior can be foreseen.

MASK, PERSON, AND VALUE

Personality reduced to a mask would be only a heap of objective qualities, and this is the way many psychologists have regarded it, since it is so difficult to define the subject in terms of subject. Classifications of character are ordinarily based on the postulate that each combination of main psychic traits forms a different human type or formula. This postulate is convenient; but what it really yields is a classification of masks and not a science of personalities as such, which it would be naive to conceive in this fashion. The complexity and mobility of masks are such that efforts to catalog them will always be disappointing. The most useful indications in this area will necessarily be limited to broad categories: for example, Jung rightly distinguishes the introvert and the extrovert types corresponding to the predominance of the interior or the exterior masks in the conscious personality.

But when we try to unmask consciousness and reach personality itself, precisely what are we looking for? The Arabs compare the self to an onion that has to be peeled layer by layer; and one may wonder whether, after revealing a deeper intention beneath the mask, this very intention may not have to be regarded as a more subtle mask. Where should we stop in this process? And do not the depths of being always escape our ken? Is there a *nucleus* of personality? Suppose that beneath the affability of a visitor I discover a selfish request; do I have the right to identify this man with his ruse? Is he entirely in the selfishness that impelled him toward me? I have discovered only one aspect of him: an immediate intention which is not his total self. No doubt, a self is indivisible and, in a sense, reveals itself entirely in its passing act. However, this self is a totality in the process of becoming; it can change its course. On the one irreplaceable theme that is its personal originality, it can weave new variations very different from those that preceded or will follow! Neither does the self yield itself any more in its spontaneous appearance than in its exterior mask, neither is it in its interior mask, i.e., in the present expression it chooses. "I am" means, "I move about, I seek my self and never grasp it."

Upon reflection, however, this uncertainty is dissipated. Of course, the deepest self will never be discovered as one discovers the seed in the center of the fruit. While the self is always incomplete, it is at the same time in all its momentary choices. Each time I act, the choice I make creates values which emanate from my act; they form a host of self-images which assimilate and integrate natural qualities derived from my heredity and environment; their meeting is my fulfillment in history, the work of my personification in my journey in time. But my range of choices is necessarily dependent on an initial value that is neither my work nor that of an impersonal nature, nor even of other human persons, but God's creative will in me. This value, which I always find before me when I try to grasp myself, is my ideal in its most inalienable form; it is the basis of my absolute originality. No mater what I do, I shall never escape the call that already confers a consistency and a particular style on my most scattered efforts. My vocation to be total requires that I become unique, and, inversely, I shall not be unique except by becoming total.

To conquer myself, I must enter with the universe into a relationship of reciprocal knowledge and action. This goal obliges me to express myself in a process and unify myself in a variety of temporal acts. Thus I am present to myself in all my actions, and I must find myself again in each one of them if I want to find their meaning. Each expression of myself in time supposes a positive self that aims at an ideal value—an ideal value that requires my positive self. I am an active freedom by my absolute vocation, and these two terms likewise define me without the possibility of their being separated from each other. It follows that each new decision I make appears to me either as an interior mask or as the substance of my being, depending on whether I place the accent on my vocation or on my fulfillment. My ideal tends to be positive, and my positive act tends to become for me a borrowed garment, a passing function, the prelude of my beauty to come. However, I am in both of these two aspects, and the depth of my being is in their union.

But am I equally in each of these two aspects? If my vocation is to fully attain my self by myself to the point of being able to deny my vocation to a certain degree, my acts in time, no matter how closely joined or incoherent they may be, will always be recognizable in my vocation and will express a minimum of my particular affirmative essence. However, certain acts will express my agreement with it more fully: the ones by which I freely will the perfection of my freedom. Thus there will be some acts that tend to absorb my interior mask into my being and others that tend to separate it from it. Or, more exactly, there will be some acts that will cause my being to shine through my mask and others that will render the mask more opaque. The perfect unity of my being is never the refusal of my variety or the affirmation of an empty and unreceptive form. It is not measured by quantitative rules but by an agreement of a finer quality between the question and the answer that I constantly am to myself in the course of my inevitable and irreversible destiny.

Now, among the acts that simplify me while enriching me—and consequently best reveal me to myself—I must give first place to manifestations of love. Each time I turn myself toward other selves to love them, I simultaneously unify and enlarge the world of spirits. Within my being I make a clearing in the area of *I-Self* relation, i.e., between the interior mask and the person itself; furthermore, I open a bright passage from the interior mask to the exterior one and, finally, from the loving person to the person loved. For to love is so to orient the workings of mental or inter-mental life that one and the same ray can traverse them both in a straight line. To this effect love will certainly use as much as necessary the various meanders indicated in our discussion of Masks and the I-Thou Relation. None of them is forbidden to it, and it sometimes requires the lover to withdraw in silence or hide from the eyes of the loved one. But behind the auxiliary structure of the masks, love always aims at unmasking the lover while unmasking the beloved, and at establishing mutual confidence and surrender between them. This transparent, central connection is not at the end of a technique but at the heart of a mutual gift. Hence, each one can comply with his natural situation and adjust the lights and shadows: *Da quod jubes et jube quod vis. . . .*

In love, since the ideal of the *I* is the value of the *thou,* the inner and outer continuity of center of consciousness is immediately acquired in principle by their will to mutual promotion. Whatever the complexity of their work in nature may be, the lover and the beloved know they are united by a consent that makes them entirely knowable and interacting in the service of their supreme value; they have introduced a promise of transparency into all their acts. Alone, masks divide more than they can unite; but when the person using them conforms his choice to an ideal that proceeds definitively from God Himself, total communion of centers of consciousness is possible; a communion that illuminates and attracts the obstacle that was threatening it; a communion that abandons symbolic disguises or else penetrates them with its presence, for it moderates their disparities, and even rebellion cannot wholly ignore it. In this communion, as in a divine polyphony, each self is a song sustaining the other melodies; and all are joined together for the sake of all, in the art of creative Wisdom.

NOTES

1. Marcel Proust, *Le Temps retrouvé* (Paris, 1928). English translation by Frederick A. Blossom, *The Past Recaptured* (New York, Modern Library, 1932), p. 255. All page references are to the English edition.

2. Hairstyle and makeup, not to mention modern resources of esthetic surgery, are intermediary between the bodily mask and removable clothing.

3. In the ancient theatre the mask was used to magnify the voice and make it sound (*personare*) in the ears of the audience. At least that is what Aulus-Gellius supposed. On the etymology and exact meaning of the word *persona,* allow me to refer to my article "Prosopon et Persona dans l'antiquité classique. Essai de bilan linguistique," in the *Revue des Sciences Religieuses* XXVIII (1948), 277–99.

4. There are excellent remarks on this point in E. Utitz, *Psychologie der Simulation* (Stuttgart, 1918); *Charakterologie* (Stuttgart, 1925), pp. 266–71.

9 ❖ *The Flights of the Work from Its Creator*

Astronomers speak of a law of an expanding universe as if the order of physical structures obliged them to disperse. We note something similar in consciousness. The union of self with self, or of self with the other, and even more, of self with nature, seems destined to have only an initial and ephemeral existence, or rather, to go on and to be reborn only in a counter-flow, like stars regrouping themselves within centrifugally expanding galaxies. In all "poetic" or "practical" activity man is subject to the flight of his works. He is made by making them; but they are made by leaving him and perhaps even unmaking him. He gambles his very being in the venture.

The analysis of the idea of novelty would bring us to the same conclusion, by an indirect route. The novel is what has never been known, or more fundamentally, what has not yet been. Now, outside the subjective *cogito,* we are never certain that the present is new, or even that there is a present.

On the other hand, every present of the consciousness is evidently original: even if I am unaware of, or forget, the resemblance between a state of soul I am now experiencing and those I experienced in the past, my illusion suffices to renew me. The most mediocre human consciousness is always sheltered from the commonplace. From the moment there is an *I,* there is a spark and a genius unlike anything else. In each of its pulsations the person is aware of and feels its newness: it knows immediately that the appearance and the being of this newness are identical in it. The mind has nothing to fear from error in this field; should error appear, the consciousness would devour it and nourish the original truth with it. Evidence of this kind is proof against failures within and "evil geniuses" without.

But consciousness perceives in its very newness a need for continuity. It is constantly building its prospects on its own past and future, as well as on the world. Hence, it will introduce into its prospect a content that partially escapes the pure form of its bare subjectivity. It is not sure that its work, under this aspect, is new in the way its present form is: I can never assert, without an act of faith, that the objective side of my acts did not exist some time before, or, *a fortiori,* that a given natural reality, included in my conscious perspective, is without precedent. Thus the subject that encounters, collects, and uses the multitude of his objects, begins by stripping them of their temporal features and converting them into essences, satisfied to immerse them afterwards in an existential series where they will be assigned a date coinciding with his enterprise. No matter how far he pushes realistic audacity, he cannot set up an absolute history except at the point of his own subjectivity and by allowing a question to subsist regarding the absolute novelty of the world.

The spirit, upon objectifying itself, discovers the partial flight of the primordial work represented by the order of object. It is paradoxically stripped and isolated in the very creation it establishes in its bosom. The radical certitude coinciding with the perpetual freshness of its energy is expressed only in an ambiguous structure. The spirit diffuses its newness like a drop of blood in an ocean; but the ocean reveals to it nothing of its origin, and in the repeated offers of its own receding surfaces, prevents the spirit from reaching its true depths.

Let us trace more accurately the flight of the work from its creator. Preceding the work there is already a state of separation: since I know myself as present I know myself as a chain of disconnected acts detached from a background. When I recapture my act within my act, when I obey the creative instinct implied in the very datum of my present being, I structure my own creature. And this creature, even were it myself-for-myself, is no longer only set apart from me, it is in flight with respect to me. If I recapture my act, this retrieval, which supposes a previous, spontaneous absence from my act, exposes me to losing it again in another manner —no longer through poverty but through wealth, as a ripe fruit detaches itself from the tree after draining its sap.

Thus there are two levels of separation: one is given, the other acquired; one afflicts the consciousness being born, the other threatens the consciousness that has regained mastery of itself. Between the two a challenge is issued; for flight, even originating in the self, is provocative. But whereas the original flight marks a release of tensions practically coeval with our being, the second one is much less banal—it reveals the independence of our work; it plants an autonomous seed in action; by it, action is an operation into which the subject inserts a world of objects.

Even at this level the types of flight are extremely varied. The most personal work is in us, and it is ourself; the world of objects is at first psychic, and only the subject knows its total configuration. The current that carries along memories or desires, thoughts and images, does not separate them only from the subject they express but sets them at a distance from each other. All these essences fly off and disperse like a swarm of bees. But the current is contained; the swarm tends to regroup and dispose itself in a number of more or less stable sub-groups. Though they cannot fuse, all these elements readily communicate with and signify one another.

The mobile configuration of their encounters signifies myself to me, and their signifying power is much more complex than a projection of the subject in the object, as a rudimentary psychology once supposed. The work I construct in myself by myself is, in its most hidden circuit, a language in which I alone can fully recognize myself; it is this circuit that makes my solitude irreducible; and it is there, no doubt, that the schizophrenic completely withdraws. However, since there is work, there is exile, too. But work does not have its own consistency; it stays in the subject's orbit. Its independence is only a hesitation between the forces that separate us and the forces that reunite us. It has no other purpose than the subjective self; without that it falls back into nothingness.

Quite different is the flight of the technical work. With it, the objects remain, and their autonomy is no longer a nothingness but an active delegation of authority. Machines survive the mind that conceived them; they are realities that can produce other realities; and, in certain cases, they even kill the body that formed them—the weapon of the suicide, for example. They evolve, and their system has a coherent, irreversible history.

What is most strange is that technical separation from the creator favors communication between creators. Whereas the symbolism of pure thought is private, the symbolism of tools is public. The break with the inner life of man makes possible the mechanical cooperation of men. Once human subjects assume the risk of depersonalization and consummate it in cybernetics, they can agree on all kinds of material and even moral progress. Technical instrumentality, while setting the mind against its work, involves a virtual reconciliation of minds through their action on nature. On the periphery of their being and in the operation that most exposes them to disintegration, centers of consciousness still find a subjective, and even an intersubjective, power for self-personalization that leads homeward by a narrow but sure road.

We separated "poetic" from "practical" operation, viz., technical from immanent operation. But not without reservations. These areas are not enclosed inside neat boundaries; between them there is the bridge of language, or rather, of languages. Whether it be scientific, artistic, or commonplace, language always has two faces: it combines ineffable meanings with technical tools; it weaves in and out everywhere, and can infinitely vary the proportions of object and subject. The choice of a word is the choice of an expressive universe with numerous latent correspondences; yet we combine these universes, we constantly add new levels of expression to those we have already built.

The airy empire of words has its own devious paths, even

when it is fixed in matter and resembles a machine, as in printed forms or recorded sound. For speech, too, separates from its creator, develops its own needs, and follows an irreversible evolution. Its fertility is neither that of a soul immured in its internal signs, nor of a technical idea inscribed in a mechanical device foreign to the soul; it asserts itself in communication and endures only by passing from one human mind to another. The secession of this work is bound up with its transmission; it is nomadic and lends itself to misconception. The interval between the creative purpose and the operative result already exists in the manipulation of tools, but this is accidental to *homo faber;* in the case of *homo loquens,* the interval becomes immense and chronic. The autonomy proper to language is systematic ambiguity; it not only retreats to the rear as if it were an interior mirror, or sidewards as some technical work: it runs ahead and sets man in pursuit of the *logos.* Even mathematical language supposes crossroads, since it requires new developments. Although ambiguity is the misery of languages, it is even more their grandeur. This flight also characterizes reason: for at the core of all language is the spirit of mediation and agile negotiation.

We have included art with language, for that is all it is, despite its pretensions to be more. The work of art is, certainly, an ontological center, a quasi-person, virtually independent of its creator, just as a child is of its parents—but on condition that it be received in another consciousness or series of consciousnesses. Without spectators or listeners the most beautiful masterpieces are only incoherent material objects. The perfection of a painting or a symphony invades all their parts equally; they are more integrated than a living or thinking being. But despite the brilliant performance that sets them in the heaven of an eternally completed liberty, the painting and the symphony live at the expense of their admirers and do not subsist without them. This accounts for the greedy nature of the work of art and the fact that it often devours not only the substance of the artist, but of the art lover as well.

Finally, there is a separation that recapitulates all the others: a consciousness born of another consciousness. Here we are confronted with the mystery of interpersonal influence. Here, indeed, it is right to say, with the neoplatonic philosophers, that to transmit is to generate, and that transmission operates a kind of reversal. No doubt they were too quick to assimilate antitypism or antitropism in intellectual exchanges, with physical or logical opposition. But any interiority induced in the other self eludes the one who caused it. The success of the mother-consciousness as cause sometimes involves a renunciation that can be cruel and apparently total. Here we discover the bond between love and death. True, it is only a death for a birth; it is provisory and exists only in the loving intention. Besides, the separation in which the offspring seems to take pleasure is neither perfectly nor easily realizable. Of course, in the act by which it comes into existence, the new creature usually presents itself without reference to its origins. Autonomy initially implies forgetfulness and ingratitude; dazzled by the immediate and obvious fact of its being, subjective newness seeks nothing but itself. However, it is anchored in its causes and cannot escape them dialectically, for they are present to it in the form of its interior growth.

Reciprocity of minds is ontologically and psychologically necessary, even for the one who rejects it and steels himself against it. The *I* needs reciprocity to be itself; it recognizes it in the will's finality, after having perhaps excluded it from the awareness of its cause. No one wills himself without rejoining the beings from whom he proceeds. At the beginning and the end there is no longer any flight of conscious selves, though it does exist in all the intervening experiences, in the form of a slowing down and obscuring of the creative flux. Even revolt and anarchy do not go beyond their preambles; they are limited processes in the mental, if not in the physical order.

The paradox of flight in this case is as follows: when one consciousness influences another, the gift of the mother-consciousness is often unknown or unrecognized by the daughter-consciousness in proportion as the gift is more primitive and causes a self to be more radically self-aware. The effectiveness of the creator and the ignorance of the beneficiary seem to be proportionate to each other. But is this not also proof that at the beginning the effectiveness is not so complete as it seems, and that a denial of effectiveness is perceptible in it? Perfect intersubjective causality cannot be reduced to a birth. If the relationship between spirits evolves according to the norms of its ontological impulse, it will eventually arrive at a mutual recognition of the past, i.e., at a present bond in which all is proposed and nothing imposed. Each one finally recreates the being whom he receives and the being who receives him. In this circumincession, the interval implied in filiation is suppressed, and we pass on to a dyadic mode of living in subjective newness. Cause and time are overthrown: cause is no longer unilateral or brutal, it becomes an unfailing harmony; time is no longer intermittent succession but an endless enfolding, gathering the whole world together, instead of dissociating it.

The reciprocal task is of two kinds, each with its own destiny. a) Insofar as it is a series of events caused by centers of consciousness, the mutual work detaches itself from the source like a trajectory, and takes on the compact, fixed character of a work of art: we can contemplate it and find personal glory or shame in it, but it remains indifferent to us. It is incapable of subsisting without the glances it receives, yet totally absorbed in its self-symbolism as an organic whole. b) On the other hand, insofar as the intersubjective work is both of the subjects themselves, it maintains much more complex relations with its creators. It is no longer a question of the "education" of a form but of the "education" of a person and even of two persons by each other. In this action each partner involves the other and creates himself. We can discern here a network of many subtle kinds of operation (thou by me and I by thee; but also thou by thyself and I by myself). This goes beyond the drama of artistic creation; the human partners have other bonds than those existing between the sculptor and his statue. In the orbit of their encounters, they can love each other and hate each other; they can despise the artisan of their being (a thing of which a statue would be incapable), and press to the limit the coexistence of their indebtedness and aggressiveness. The inexhaustible multitude of interpsychological attitudes is involved in this adventure; history and literature will never complete the inventory, for the content has been ceaselessly renewed ever since the human species began. The basic theme of the dyad remains; the variations built on it are limitless.

What would happen if, instead of an influence, there were the total presence of another conscious self? If the Creator is divine, the conscious creature always remains in His hand. But at the same time it receives the capacity to flee, more than any other work ever fled from any other creator. I am simultaneously imprisoned by and desperately separated from Him who draws me from nothingness; even before I try to get away I am exiled from His power by a kingdom of shadows unless He raises me to Himself in an incomprehensible way. My independence is, however, only a taut and controlled dependence. The liberty I receive, even should I wish to appropriate it to myself to the very limits of the absurd, is only a false exit. I am a work that escape leads back to its principal creator, for all roads lead back to the point of departure, provided one follows them to the end. This priority of God, attested to by the failure of the escape, insinuates into the wandering soul the hope of a mutuality that would engender God in man. The disparity of imposed liberty is reduced in proposed liberty and resolved in divinized liberty; such is the order of the gift, and such is, perhaps, the destination of distance.[1]

NOTES

1. A complementary study could be devoted to the flight of the creator before his work. It, too, would include many forms: from horror before the consequences ("I didn't mean that . . .") or disgust with a work once it is finished, to the abnegations of the educator and the silent interrogation that listens to the creature.

The worker is made by making his work. But a distinction must be drawn between the formation of self by *poiesis* and the aftereffect of the *poiema.*

10 ✦ Is There Reciprocity of Centers of Consciousness in History?

In a certain sense, the study of history begins when the reciprocity of minds ends and communication between them is no longer possible. As long as we live with other men and work as a team with them, our subjective or intersubjective certitudes are not, properly speaking, historical; for the other answers us and we answer him, we can verify our hypotheses about him and ourselves by the reactions we excite in each other. But as soon as a space or time interval between minds becomes so great that they lose their mutual contact, the knowledge we acquire of the unfolding of subjective life takes on the character of history. At that moment the interlocutor ceases to reply; there remains only our monologue before documents whose limited and, as it were, frozen mass, contains all the secrets we can decipher. Such is evidently the situation in which the past places us, especially if death has carried off the actors in the drama under study and definitively withdrawn them from our vital synchronism.

Such even is our situation in the face of current events, when geography or society locates them too far from us: thus the speech of a statesman read in the paper or heard on the radio by an ordinary citizen immediately takes on a historical character because the statesman is inaccessible to the ordinary citizen.

History, by definition, involves a paradoxical effort: it pretends to maintain the absent as present; it pursues persons who withdraw; it tries to recover in solitude a community that is physically out of reach.[1]

This very desire of the historian probably flows from his need to understand himself. Our consciousness is not our whole being, and we feel it has been prepared or formed by forces of the past whose precise nature escapes us. I want to be aware of my responsibilities, master my unconscious, know whence I came. This search in the obscure regions of my person naturally leads me to the science of the body; but I do not depend only on my molecules, I also depend on the centers of consciousness that preceded or protected mine. When I retrace this last path, I construct history; even were I doing so to understand the structure of my molecules, I would be looking for what they owe to the existence of minds either unknown or no longer present. This reconstruction requires that I go beyond the line of my parents or ancestors. By subtle and more or less indirect projections in which the points of arrival serve as new points of departure, I explore the past of my ethnic group, I am linked to a chain of civilizations. "Know thyself": is this not the deepest reason, and in any case the most honorable one, for teaching our children about the existence of Louis XIV or the Cro-Magnon man?

Although it is regressive, history thus conceived is ego-centric. It is also explicative, since its purpose is to explain us to ourselves. But after having traveled back from the present which constitutes us, or which we perceive in the invisible past that enlightens us, history returns to us from this past, which it binds to itself in order to bind it to us. We discover our causes, then observe the panorama of their consequences, ourselves included. Analytic explanation is followed by a synthesis in which each event evokes another and the whole shows the general shape of the past.

However, these various modes of explanation are not homogeneous. Besides, we must not regard the past that we take as the matter of our investigation, as a chain of links that might have been perfectly conscious and intentionally directed toward us. Men have succeeded one another here below without clearly willing their succession; their projects have been ceaselessly crossed by the contingencies of nature. Even when they intended what happened, they did not do us the honor of thinking of us by name, since we were unforeseeable to them. Has there been any conscious continuity from them to us? Was there even any continuity between themselves? Yes, certainly, in the interior of the same generation, or at the juncture of two generations. But how often are not men, gathered together in space and time in the same destiny, ignorant of one another! Along the road whose goals and detours they do not foresee, they are more anxious about others than acquainted with them. When there actually is reciprocity, it consists (especially for heads of states) more in mutual challenges and explosive misunderstandings than in love. In a word, in the documentary film of the past, the isolation of minds is seemingly more apparent and operative than their continuity.

Thus, if the historian seeks a field of reality furrowed with brilliant achievements and persuasive dialogues, he will be disappointed. This is not the way to explain the past or ourselves by means of the past. He must replace the consciousness of men in nature's flowing stream and substitute a sufficiently chronological description for a very intelligible explanation. Thus it is a matter of filling in the frame of time with facts, without leaving any empty centuries, if possible. Where intellectual cohesion is lacking, we hope for factual completeness. Of its ambition to explain all, history thence retains only a desire of empiric totality. Its objective is to be able to say "what happened," i.e., all that prepared our arrival in the course of each period.

Even this more modest presentation is doomed to failure. The progress of historical science implies the inadequacy of integral explication, if that word is used in its etymological sense of a simple *unfolding* of decisive facts. For we cannot recount everything; we extract only a small part of the past, the part that the survival of documents saves from objective destruction. Thus, the more experienced the historian is, the more he must forego the popular picture-book illustrations with their all-inclusive horizons. He notes bitterly that the relief map we draw of the past is deceptive, owing largely to our ignorance. What has become of the miracle of Greek geometry, for example, since the discovery of the Sumerian inscriptions? The unearthing of a few clay fragments suffices to change the profile of a thousand years.

The need of an explanatory whole is, nevertheless, at the heart of history and cannot be eliminated from it. While we are quite satisfied with the current circle of our intersubjective relations and do not pretend to reduce the rest of humanity to the little island of our private experience, the moment we look back to the past we are seized with the ambition to make all its reality gravitate around the past that we have reconstructed. The thirst to know everything engenders the illusion that we have examined everything. It is impossible to assuage this thirst, but we must get rid of this illusion. The only way to succeed is by a Copernican revolution: in place of the history that pretends to explain our appearance and nature, we must substitute a history that is turned toward the conscious beings of the past, whoever they may be, take them as centers, and be interested in them for their own sake.

In this more centrifugal concept of research the historian is no longer concerned as to whether such and such a past event did or did not have any influence on the present. He totally renounces egocentric concern and contemplates the object in itself. He thereby introduces it immediately as an active force in our contemporary world. For the first time, perhaps, a particular person of the past, unknown and ineffective in his time, will be included in the activities of the human centers of consciousness that have followed him. He will enter there directly, in full daylight, since he will do so as a result of our conscious investigation. He will reach *Geschichte* by way of *Historie.* In this connection we naturally think of the resurrection of certain personalities through the anecdote. But it is not only a question of giving a little celebrity, as an afterthought, to a few characters without breadth, or shut up in an enclave far from the highways of their time. It is not even a question of the exceptional glories accorded very late to a J. S. Bach or a Kierkegaard. The phenomenon we have in mind is much more general: all the minds of the past are, ultimately, in the same situation, insofar as they are studied by today's scholars and replaced in the contemporary stream to exercise a posthumous and reflex influence. The original journey of these men in the humanity that preceded us matters little; they are beginning a new destiny in us through the awareness we have of their consciousness; we know that this aspect of them that we contemplate is the term of a new act by which we confer on them a kind of hitherto unpublished life. For them, as for us, a relationship is established that might be regarded as truly reciprocal, although they did not foresee this encounter and we do not have the means, by definition, to modify their past in their past.

If we practice history this way, we escape the vicious circle in which we usually enclose the relation of *Geschichte* and *Historie.* At first it seems that these notions can neither be really separate nor satisfying. What we have received from the past (*geschichtlich*), secretly insinuates itself into our manner of studying it (*historisch*); whence the fear we have of being incapable of impartiality in our judgments. The physicist's mentality certainly cannot be carried over into a method in which we never know on what influences we depend nor what their subjective survival in us may be.[2] On the other hand, our study of the past never adequately reproduces what it was, and we do not know whether the relative importance of factors was, in past reality, what it is in our present reconstruction; this subjects the image of the centuries to incessant remodelings. Every work of history is thus exposed to the reproach of being partial, both in the sense of incomplete and in the sense of biased.

But suppose our historian ceases to pursue the impossible dream of projecting behind himself a total objectivity and a subjective totality; suppose he keeps only the need of being open to the encounter of any consciousness that enriches and universalizes his own. At that very moment it becomes possible for him to escape the antinomies of *Geschichte* and *Historie* which were impeding the realization of the explicative ideal. Why, indeed, would one accuse our historian of bias? He has the right to contemplate a personality of the past and study him as if he were a friend he discovers and chooses in virtue of their mutual affinities.[3] And how can he be blamed for being incomplete when he makes no pretense of telling all? He does not claim to exhaust the series of significant facts or examine all the causes leading to the present world and terminating, finally, in his own active subjectivity. His point of departure is, on the contrary, that active subjectivity just as it is given to him, and he involves past subjectivities with him in a common adventure.

He must work more than ever with a maximum of objectivity and seek what those minds, to which he now clings, were originally in the past. But if he wishes to know what they were, it is in order to give to them, as to living persons, an unlooked-for opportunity to influence him as he is and perhaps to jolt him a bit in order to help him fulfill himself. Thus there is between them and him a kind of collaboration and an acquired reciprocity in which he exercises the initiative.

While distinguishing two concepts of history, the egocentric and the centrifugal, we did not say that the first should surrender its place to the second, for without the first it would be impossible to arrive at the second. Were it not for the need for regressive explanation, we could not acquire the notion of an objective series of facts. But what the second concept of history rejects in the first is the pretension to explain everything and suppress the mystery of human becoming. It is enough if centrifugal history achieves a partial objectivity and occasionally discovers the presence of personalities in documents, just as one detects a soul in three or four lines of a portrait. Balfour maintained, and rightly so, that the past has a fibrous constitution; and Bergson held that a limited certitude could be absolute.

Fifty years ago there was much discussion about the "Christ of history" and the "Christ of faith." In a sense less technically bound to exegesis and theology, we might also speak of a "Socrates of history" and a "Socrates of faith." In other words, each time a person with a spiritual message is involved, there is a perspective of history and a perspective of faith. The first is scientific and explicative; the second, artistic and comprehensive.

Are these not merely two forms of the same object? We might be tempted to think so, but this is really not the case. History and faith can never be completely separated. We cannot tear ourselves away from what we are in order to materially touch the past. What is true is that there is a rational use and an impassioned use of our subjectivity. As a consequence, there is a serious history and a fantastic one, a shrewd faith and a foolish one. In speaking of regressive explanation and centrifugal contemplation we were far from opposing history and faith. In explanation, as in contemplation, there is a factual outlook and a belief; these two can no more be dissociated than can a luminous object and the focusing of the eye in visual perception. But it is true that in another sense the two forms of history correspond to two different levels of research. On the one hand we want to enclose Socrates or Christ in the chain of the past that produces us and in which they are links. On the other, we seek less to reconstruct the past integrally in the past than to extract documentary evidence from it for meditation and action in the present. What we have received from the past does, indeed, obscurely influence our manner of studying it, but this osmosis ceases to be dangerous in the centrifugal concept of history.

It will be helpful to conclude by determining more explicitly the psychic reciprocities that are met in history.

1) Mention should be made, in the first place, of the reciprocities binding men together during the same epoch and whose forms, of an interpsychological or sociological order, vary to some degree with human evolution. They constitute an undeniable historical factor, even though the past is made up not only of interpsychic relations, more or less clearly intentional, but also of material events.

2) Each generation communicates its existence to the one following. Predecessors influence their successors not only by heredity or education but by institutions, exchanges, etc. This heritage is not perpetual since, in the course of time, mementos are lost and mutations frequently occur. We nevertheless bear within ourselves sentiments and images that bind us to the past and which, furthermore, turn us deliberately toward it, at least in a global manner (e.g.,

patriotic feeling). In this case one may certainly speak of a reciprocity of the unconscious, if not of the conscious.

3) Abstracting from spontaneous relationships of this kind, we can ask whether a particular reciprocity is conceivable between personages of the past and the historian who studies them.

At first glance it would not seem so. Are not our partners of former times separated from us by absence or death? Plato used to call the plastic arts the "arts of silence." Could the same not be said of history? However, the silence of a work of art is itself a special message from the past; it is a kind of intentional document. Intersubjectivity is not annihilated as long as there is a material inscription and, above all, a technical inscription such as art or writing. Every document really proves that to live is to be held up to the gaze of others and to possible examination in the future. To consent to live is, for a thinking individual, to be intentionally directed toward all the other thinking individuals, at least insofar as one is exposed to leaving traces of oneself that other eyes may gaze upon some day.

4) Hence, if we try to explain what we are today, we will shed light on the obscure aspects of our personal being, not through the biological unconsciousness of the species only, but more precisely through the conscious beings of the past and their influence on us. The documents we read may reveal that these persons of times past acted unconsciously on the *Geschichte*. But a new reciprocity will unite us to the persons of history when we become aware of what they were, even though in this relationship their attitude does not coincide with ours and the encounter is, by hypothesis, imperfect.

5) This encounter will gain in purity if the historian

renounces the excessive ambition of reconstituting all past personalities within his own past and strives to study them for themselves insofar as he can discover them. To attach himself thus to their otherness is to will to discover them as exactly as possible and offer them, in addition, a new life in his present.

Although history thus conceived reminds us of Plutarch's *Lives of Famous Men* and seems more ethical than scientific, it is really the only way to reconcile *Geschichte* and *Historie,* because it offers to the past a new life in the present, and for this very purpose must seek the truth of the past in the past because of the greater exigency of the present. To reflect upon the likeness of a dead person, to discover him as he was in life, is to give him life in ourselves; the life coming to him through us will be truly his. This is the highest degree of reciprocity possible to history. Thanks to it, the majesty of death can reinforce the disinterestedness of love. But this kind of spiritual communion is halting and effected only through artifice. When our consciousness fixes its intention on a person of the past, the latter is only an effluvium, and reaches us as such. Unaware of the lot we create for them, the souls of the dead are active dreams. Like works of art, their existence is in our hands, but their essence is from beyond and observes us. Thus history amplifies the stratification of personal exchanges here below, preventing them from being perfectly simultaneous, equally explicit, or identically directed toward one another.

6) There remains the question of reciprocity between historians. We have not taken up this question because historians are men, and their situation would send us back to categories previously examined. But beyond professional

communication, the historian probably remains alone before the past, like the artist before beauty and the philosopher before the world.

NOTES

1. There are many kinds of histories; I am here considering only the history of centers of consciousness. At least I shall consider the others only insofar as they concern this one. But it is evident that this is not the only one or the most common one. It should be noted that each type of history requires different qualities of intelligence and method. Battles are not studied in the same manner as institutions, nor do we use the same procedure to trace the course of ideas and the development of a national economy.

2. No doubt when a twentieth-century Frenchman is studying Aztec civilization he has a greater intellectual freedom than when he is studying the Revolution of 1789 or the government of Marshal Pétain. But since he lacks internal references for the former he is not better off for all his freedom.

3. That is, a complex affinity which is not always a facile sympathy. It is what permits an adversary to be just to his enemy and a scholar to become enthusiastic about a cause that is really indifferent or repugnant to him.

11 ❖ *Thought and Life in the Transmission of Philosophical Doctrines*

Abstracting from the relation between life and thought in the actual formation of philosophical doctrines, I should like to treat only of their transmission or dissemination. At the very outset it appears that their diffusion is owing not only to the truth or logical force of the ideas, but quite as much, if not more, to their appearance, or even their falseness. Do you want to popularize an idea? Cloak it in a sophism, rather than in right reason—you will give it more surface appeal and immediate interest. This observation not only obliges us to distinguish the *in itself* and the *for us* of doctrines (i.e., the ideas themselves and their formulation); it obliges us also to study the living milieu in which the doctrines are propagated (i.e., inter-human relations in space and time).

In other words, the relation of thought to life in this area cannot be reduced to an interior and an exterior of the idea (insofar as the idea has, on the one hand, its own private economy and, on the other, an analyzable aspect). It is not even a question of reducing everything to a relation of thought to thinker (insofar as the thinker would remain a kind of disembodied spirit whose substance would be nothing but the act of thinking). We must go farther and recognize that thinkable doctrines can be separated from the men who transmit them; the latter are then more or less rapid and more or less faithful vehicles. Thus understood, life is a transmitter that offers to thought either services or obstacles of a material, psychic, or social order.

The initial dissemination of a doctrine is explained schematically and roughly by the interaction of three practically equal causes: the personality of the philosopher, his social life, and the money at his disposal (particularly for the purpose of publishing). Each of these causes should, of course, be subdivided. The personal factor, for example, is complex: originality of intelligence is certainly not the most effective element. Also to be considered is a kind of radiant energy, a mysterious something that at one time seems to be essentially feminine and ingratiating (physical charm, grace of expression, adaptability and fellow-feeling, the lure of a certain attractive obscurity), at another, masculine and intimidating (aggressiveness in manner and voice, forcefulness of assertion and mental suggestion, etc.). The greatest genius in the world depends largely on these natural characteristics which, though independent of his intelligible message, guarantee it a good start in time.

The thinker has a milieu. Thinker and milieu form the two variables of all success. The atmosphere through which the doctrine passes is more or less prepared to receive it.

That is why there are late comers and precursors, or, contrariwise, "sounding echoes" in perfect euphoric accord with their surroundings. That, too, is why there are two modes of philosophical success: by conquest and by crystallization.

Kant is an example of the first type. The only thing he had in his favor was the general weariness with the *Aufklärung;* people needed a change; Wolff was becoming tiresome and Kant himself was to grow weary of commenting on Baumeister. Thus the triumph of criticism was immediate and prodigious. It was not, however, a triumph gained in fierce battle: Kant had only Crusius against him. But he has not carried along by a set current of opinion, and in this sense he conquered his place in the sun. On the other hand, Schelling responded to the romantic expectation of the new century; he crystallized the lyricism of Europe in his philosophy. Like Kant, he immediately had his commentators in Moscow as well as in Paris, but his philosophy of nature and the soul was already in the air, whereas Kant brought something unforeseeable. The one filled a vacuum by creating a new form, the other bent and amplified a form already half complete.

According to circumstances, an author benefits from the fact that an idea is in the air, that is to say, the idea is prepared without having yet been proffered; or, also, from the fact that the idea has never been conceived and fills a free space, as one takes an empty seat in a railroad car; or, finally, from the fact that the opposite idea has been dominating opinion for so long that men are beginning to abandon it in favor of something new.[1]

Life offers a field or space for a doctrine to travel through. This distance can be geographical or cultural. In the latter case the idea must pass through linguistic, institutional, or ideological barriers. Are there any laws for these various penetrations?

In itself geographical distance has no influence on doctrine. If a thought is frequently altered in transit, it is because it has to pass through a cultural distance. It can meet this obstacle in some form at home. As soon as it has to pass from one language to another, enter into another intellectual tradition, etc., the old axiom is at once verified: *quidquid recipitur ad modum recipientis recipitur.*

We have just cited the example of Kant. It would be a fascinating thing to show what happened to him as he traveled through Europe. Mme de Stael read him through Jacobi's glasses; Bautain made a voluntarist of him; Renouvier suppressed his noumenon and put him to work for the philosophy of relation.[2] In England, Coleridge and Carlyle congratulated him on having made skepticism impossible and risen above the seductions of matter, space, and time: for them, Kant reincarnated Plato. Hamilton, on the contrary, regarded him as an Aenesidemus, while Edward Caird sought in his books a kind of dialectic on the march, a Hegelian system before the time. All qualified him on the score of their religious hopes. In Italy, Rosmini rejected Kant as a sophist whose synthetic *a priori* judgment contains the germ of all later idealism and of that German philosophy which is "intent on mocking man and making him constantly oscillate between nothingness and all."[3] In Spain, Balmès' attack was more vehement still.

In brief, England and France transformed Kant in order to adapt him to their national traditions, while the southern countries banished him in an effort to maintain theirs. Whether he was attacked, or welcomed into the bosom of the family, it cannot be said he was generally understood. A man's thought is distorted in proportion to its success.

This conclusion is all the more correct when success is owing to a crystallization. What does Victor Cousin's Schelling have in common with the Schelling of Lammenais, Ravaisson, Charles Secrétan or, particularly, of Tschaaden and the occidentalist Russians? Wherever his thought is received, it gives the impression of a truncated work, about to fall apart. In short, the greater the cultural distance traversed by a philosophy, the more it is deformed. It stimulates the minds that receive it, but this fecundity is paid for by misinterpretation to the point that in the end it becomes the contrary of what it was in the beginning.

This state of things is easy to explain. When an author is famous, his success is contagious; but beyond a certain degree of amplitude success is always a crystallization. After that, intelligent disciples and conscientious critics are no longer of any help to him. Instead of a diffusion of philosophy among philosophers, we are treated to a literary or social adventure, or a mass phenomenon. In the end, his fellow-craftsmen learn from the crowd what is happening to one of their number. What results may be an emulation of sorts, but not a guarantee of exactitude. If the successful author, who has achieved such glory, has genius, there will not be the slightest chance of his work's eliciting objective commentaries during his lifetime. Genius suffices to make a doctrine too moving and exuberant to be correctly perceived, except at a distance in time.

We have just sketched a theory of *immediate* success. What would be the relation between thought and life when the propagation of the message is deferred?

a) We call *deferred* the success that passes through the intermediary of a generation of disciples. This is usually the academic way: a doctrine, accepted at the University by the students, reaches the secondary and elementary schools when these students teach in their turn. It can thus be extended to important sectors of the nation. Sometimes opinion effects a similar progress in relays. In this respect we might compare the rising curve of Nietzsche and Durkheim.

The conjunction of life and thought offers nothing really new with reference to the preceding case, except that it often involves a time of eclipse between the first appearance of the system and its adoption by a second generation of disciples. The risks of deformation in this situation are considerable, especially under the form of scholastic sclerosis. There is a curious law to the effect that commentaries on commentaries are always false constructions. Without direct contact with the author's text a gloss inevitably leads to an error.

The example of Hegel, whose success was deferred in several countries, would confirm, with chronological adjustments, what we noted with regard to Kant and Schelling. Thus, soon after Hutchison Stirling's private lectures, and the formation of a group of Hegelian faithful, with the publication of the *Essays in Philosophical Criticism* (1883), the knell of independence was struck for Hegel in Great Britain. The disciples went off in three directions: along with intelligent but unfruitful commentaries like Wallace's, there developed a personal idealism of the Pringle-Pattison type, or a mystical Spinozism of the Nettleship variety. Then freedom of interpretation increased further with Bradley, Bosanquet, and MacTaggart. These Anglo-Hegelians are decidedly much more English than Hegelian, and their absolute does not resemble in the least the becoming of the

Italo-Hegelian, such as Croce or Gentile, As for Germany itself, Feuerbach and Marx evidently did more for the glory of the master than Rosenkranz—but with what infidelity!

b) I would call *tardy* a success that follows a period of silence or incubation of more than a half century, i.e., several generations, if we accept Thibaudet's idea that there are three literary generations to a century, or, all the more so, if we accept Henri Peyre's who counts one almost every fifteen years.[4] We must admit that this notion of a "literary generation" is not very clear, given the mixture of influential men of very different ages at any given time.

A tardy success is really an exhumation, or, if one prefers a less macabre term, a resurrection. Kierkegaard is a good example of this. Unrecognized during his lifetime (1813–1855), he was an author of but little local fame, hampered by his non-diffusive language and by the fact that he was on the sidelines of the philosophical trends of his time; he was going against the current. Nevertheless, an edition of his *Samlede Vaerker* came out in fourteen volumes in Copenhagen, and he had a little circle of admirers in Germany at the beginning of the twentieth century. But until around 1920 the articles or books written about him could be counted on one's fingers: in Spain, Unamuno studied Danish so that he could read him in the original; in France, in 1900, H. Delacroix wrote an article about him in the *Revue de Métaphysique et de Morale;* in England, Baron von Hügel devoted several pages to him in his *Mystical Element of Religion.* Then, after the first World War and especially after 1930, there was a general explosion. He had an astounding success, and complete translations appeared in several languages seventy-five years after his death.

This is a very enviable destiny. A late success in a cultural setting that remains sufficiently homogeneous might be considered a formula for celebrity that reconciles the desire to be known for what one is with the desire to enrich other minds. The loss of vital contact with the author allows his doctrine to be appreciated with impartiality. Passions have subsided, and the reader is detached from the author's milieu, at least insofar as it was ephemeral and distorting. However, to revive an author, the mediation of experts is and will continue to be necessary. Good critical editions and conscientious commentaries are both indispensable and possible. Here notoriety no longer invites betrayal. Whereas immediate success (i.e., usually, misinterpretation) is a nervous phenomenon, exactitude is a reflective one.

True, the interpretation of Kierkegaard remains problematic; it differs according to the importance given to his *Journal* and the meaning given to his pseudonymous writings. But the enigma does not come from our prejudices; it is inherent in the very particular style intentionally cultivated by the writer. Therefore this does not constitute an objection.

c) A *very late* success, however, (for example, after an interval of several centuries) would again make misinterpretation very probable. An enormous amount of work is required to recover a mentality belonging to such a distant past. While it is more than ever necessary, scholarly mediation now attains its end only with difficulty. Even authors whose thousand-year-old glory has not been seriously interrupted—an Aristotle, a St. Augustine, for example—can be directly approached only through their psychological or logical notations; their representation of the external world escapes us for the most part, and their very anthropology, if not their metaphysics, is affected by it.

In summary, the diffusion curve of a doctrine in cultural space implies increasing diffractions and deformations.[5] But the same cannot be said of its diffusion curve in *time:* initially parallel to the first, it has a special point of inflexion in the case of late successes; then it finally succumbs to the drift inherent in extreme distance between minds.

These few remarks lead to the conclusion that life tends most often to break the communion of thinkers, and the progress of a philosophy is rarely pure or purely philosophic. It is true that to oppose life and thought is rather artificial, since there is a thought-life. It would be more correct to say that *some* forms of life harm thought. Among these forms can surely be counted the immediate conformities of opinion. In this sense the philosopher ought to fear the marketplace. Not that it is deplorable in itself that several or even many persons should think alike. But as a matter of fact, given the concrete conditions that spatio-temporal encounters or social cadres impose on us, a truly creative dialogue can be established only between a small number of minds. Far from favoring the exchange of points of view and understanding among men, massive success may bring on isolation and a kind of creeping silence.

A philosophy that is too widely diffused impedes and impoverishes truth, because the collective soul is never creative: it is limited to transmitting ideas, sometimes preserving them, most often debasing them. Fundamentally there are no collective ideas; there are only roundtable discussions among traders of ideas, and the manner of manipulating these ideas impresses an epiphenomenal form on them. If the role of popular systems is important, if the misunderstandings they provoke are fertile in the history of philosophy, it is because there are original minds for whom the reigning opinions serve as raw material or occasional causes. But to this violent and ultimately anarchic development, how preferable would be the technique for transmission that Socrates bequeathed to the Occident and which supposes a small number of interlocutors who could give one another an opportunity to speak, without the transmission of thought impeding personal invention or personal invention prohibiting the reciprocity of minds! Only the discipline that inspired this technique can reconcile life and thought in a single historical moment. It alone offers philosophers the possibility of going beyond the monologue which is their natural condition.

NOTES

1. On this point see Newman's analysis in *Essay on Development* or Tarde's on logical dueling and coupling in his *Lois de l'imitation.*

2. He later recognized that the maneuver was artificial and that he would have done better to take Descartes as his patron. See H. Méry, *La Critique du christianisme chez Renouvier,* II (Paris, 1953).

3. R. Jolivet, *De Rosmini à Lachelier* (Paris-Lyons, 1953), p. 172.

4. See P. Mesnard, *Le Cas Diderot* (Paris, 1952), pp. 9–12. Berenson shortens the lapse of time still more, writing in his *Italian Painters of the Renaissance* (Oxford, 1930) that artistic generations do not go beyond ten years. Perhaps this would be identifying "generation" and style—in this instance, style and price index among the art dealers.

5. A. Toynbee remarks in this regard that "the penetrative power of a strand of cultural radiation is usually in inverse ratio to this strand's cultural value." (*The World of the West,* Oxford, 1953, p. 68.) He adds that detached elements often act as pathogenic forces.

12 ✧ *The Intellectual Poverty of the Collective Becoming and Its History*

Man, as Hegel sees him, realizes his humanity only through an evolution in time and a progressive awareness of this evolution. History, despite its crises, weaves a continuous web in which the victory of the spirit is manifest. This spirit is not beyond and above individuals; neither does it fulfill itself in the individual alone or in a simple relationship between individuals; it sets up a whole collective organization whose forms, while apparently annihilating individual liberty, really deepen it, so that social complexity is expressed in each person, and each person finds in social complexity access to his own value.

Collective movement, according to Hegel, cannot stop at a limited expression. The family or the city, for example, cannot satisfy its *élan*. Consequently, the human being must invent wider frames of existence to help him better discover

189

himself. Since this is so, should not socialization tend to a final structure of planetary proportions? Hegel does not go to that extreme. He stops short at a plurality of rival states that are so many spiritual organisms. The dialectic progress of the human idea is elaborated in their becoming. In them the ruse of absolute reason plays with obstacles, triumphs over contingencies, and utilizes private initiatives; it rests in the ceaseless renewal of the movement it started. Thus it is principally the advent of the State and its organization that frees us and fulfills us. Thanks to the *Volksgeist,* arrived thus at maturity, each one of us receives a spiritual life whose fruit subsequently returns to the collectivity. The osmosis of the person, society, and spirit is thus realized as far as possible in the drama of time and negation.

Not everything is clear in this thesis, and uncertainties are not lacking, especially when one approaches the end and has to determine the exact relations of the State, religion, and philosophy.[1] But it does contain some themes that are indisputable and have gained the adherence of most contemporary thinkers: for example, the certitude that man realizes his humanity in history, that history expresses a dialectical necessity, and that that dialectic ends in the human reign of truth, goodness, and beauty. Similar convictions, clothed in a different vocabulary, animate both Marxist philosophers and the Christian disciples of Hegel. Both groups withdraw from the master by reason of their common aspiration toward a total or universal society positively organized beyond nations and having its own institutions. They subsequently withdraw from each other because the Marxists regard the mover and the moved in collective becoming as identical, whereas the Hegelian Christians distinguish them and suspend all time on the redemptive incarnation of Christ. But the affirmation of a dialectic progress and the attribution of a spiritual role to society are elements shared by all these anthropologies.

If we now ask the professional historians what they think of such speculations, most of them no doubt will judge them very severely. For the person who knows with what difficulty acts and their interconnections are reconstituted, such ambitious syntheses are unverifiable, or rather, overbold and false.

Thus H. Fisher declares at the beginning of his *History of Europe:* "There is an intellectual stimulation I have been refused. Better informed and more scholarly researchers than myself have discovered a plot, a rhythm, a preestablished theme in history. These harmonies have remained hidden from me." It is quite true that the sweeping frescoes of Hegel too often resemble popular color prints. He is always quick to draw out of the dark stream of the past the precise drop of water that suits his purpose. He tries to make the dialectical progress of the mind and the concrete history of nations coincide; but given our knowledge of the concrete history of nations, he must occasionally recognize their fundamental diversity.[2]

Is this to say that conscientious historians are buried in their files? Not at all. The weight of the known—and of the unknown—does not silence them to the point that they can produce no reflection on the whole. We must admit, however, that collective becoming does not seem to offer much consolation to the devotee of spiritual progress. Everything happens as if the civilizations (whose domain and chronology sometimes cut across several races) were born, grew up, and died like ill-assorted flowers that do not propagate themselves and are as irreconcilable as opposite species can be in this living world. They offer the sad spectacle of a fan-shaped diversity; they usually have no continuity and no forebears. Spengler should not be blamed for taking up Herder's ideas on this point and systematizing them as he did. Toynbee, who also counts cultural cycles and derives a nomenclature from them with more scientific competence than Spengler, seems to maintain a principle of continuity; he supposes that civilizations do not totally collapse but survive in their successors under the form of what he calls a "universal Church." But in reality this expression designates under his pen a new movement launched in the old world by a dissatisfied proletariat: thus it was with nascent Christianity in the Roman Empire. It is not a question of a global transmission but a creative antithesis. No spiritual survival is necessarily demanded by history.[3]

We should go farther and ask whether what is spiritual in the becoming of societies has a collective origin, or if what has a collective origin ever has a spiritual value. It is not the cradle that makes the child, it is not society that makes the genius of the artist, or thinker, or moralist, or scientist. Each personal destiny detaches itself from the group and raises itself in the world of its own values. No doubt the invisible conquests of these destinies can be subsequently inscribed in the group, but this is not absolutely necessary, and it is never an integral part of it. It is not true that the "within" passes entirely to the "without," as Hegel insists. The spiritual adventure, essentially personal and suprasocial, would sooner remind one of a rocket that does not necessarily return to its launching site, and, if it did, might destroy it.

Of course we cannot deny that there is a collective soul and that it precedes or prepares the rise of the person. But it is and remains below human consciousness. Far from liberating man, it holds him back in a framework of ready-made representations. The collective soul varies according to peoples and centuries; it depends on a host of racial or demographic factors; it is even graced with cultural elements. But it is not its *collective* character that explains its variety or accounts for the spiritual make-up it puts on. Quite the contrary; it is the collective character that explains what is uniform in all groups, namely, internal conservatism, brute force of expansion, and blindness as regards all values foreign to the motif of their initial type.

The opposition that Bergson sees between a society closed to spiritual values and the hero who discovers or creates them seems to be preferable to Hegel's Idea incarnate in a collectivity and constituting its system. But we should examine this problem more closely.

Our manner of presenting the facts about civilization will surely seem paradoxical and impertinent. However, while denying the spiritual dynamism of societies, we did not deny that there is such a thing as spiritual dynamism or that societies can, in a certain measure, become its depositaries. We simply refused to confuse the setting with the jewel, or, if one prefers another metaphor, the honeycomb with the honey.

Collective becoming tends to repeat its form in time and diffuse itself in space. Consequently it should have as its function to preserve values that are incarnate in a work or institution. But it cannot contain them entirely. Thus, in transmitting them it will analyze and decompose them, just as habit simultaneously transmits and weakens the free act. This sifting process also explains the facility with which certain civilizations favor now one form of culture and now another, according to the times. These efflorescences are not all possible at the same time. For example, the rise of sculpture among the Greeks, of architecture in the Middle Ages, of painting in the Renaissance, and of music in the 18th and 19th centuries has as its cause, on the one hand, an unpredictable fact: the personal presence and influence of great artists; on the other, a quite predictable fact: the impossibility of each epoch to offer a terrain equally propitious for the cultivation of all the arts. It is hazardous to seek in this development the necessary logic of a nascent idea when it is explained by the contingent distribution of private inspiration and the expressive constraints of social milieux.

Collective indigence is revealed, too, in the threat of death it unfailingly imposes on the works of the spirit, for in transmitting them it weakens them, and in exposing them it demeans them. Upon beauty, which is "a joy forever," it imposes the limits of style, i.e., liability to the fickleness of society. Schiller used to say, "The gods, too, must die," because they descend into groups whose promises are short-lived. Every civilization is hence precarious, like an electric current that depends on an outside source and meets resistance in the very metal through which it flows.

Very often this truth is not recognized. Spiritual progress is attributed to society because it is associated with a division of work. The latter is closely connected with the conditions immanent in collective becoming. It may involve the ingenuity of a leader but, on the whole, it may be explained by bio-social necessities that hasten the passage from the implicit to the explicit. When a spiritual idea falls in the group and is fixed there, it expands like a coil spring in the play of analysis and synthesis. This evolution, with its succeeding cadences, partially escapes the free will of persons. But to the degree in which it does, it offers only an appearance of novelty to each of its phases. History is filled with theories, institutions, and events linked in a chain of undeniable, age-old logic; but the spiritual sterility of these processes is only the more striking. They contribute nothing to the original germ whose virtualities they manifest.

The pseudo-progress we have just spoken of is achieved and propagated by a kind of contagious imitation or mechanical drill. True spiritual progress, on the contrary, is recognized by the fact that, challenged in each mind it penetrates, it is freely recreated and thrust farther forward, or turned in a new direction. Here we have assimilation in place of contagion, education in place of drill, and the foreshortened period of understanding for the elongated period of repetition. Perhaps we should add: the unpredictable flash of discovery in a mind that understands the other and is understood by him in the same movement, replaces the determined rhythm of an explanation imposed from without. True, the relationship between teacher and pupil begins in the framework of habit; but it is completed only when the pupil is liberated and becomes a teacher in turn. It is thus that art and philosophy, morality and mysticism, are propagated.

The same holds true for science, whose support and development are not mechanical, as one might suppose, but subject to the intermittent pulse of personal vocations.

Material successes do not necessarily engender scientific insights any more than masterpieces of art are a guarantee of the future renewal of painting. At most, they encourage the foundation of museums and academies. In the spiritual order, pseudo-progress leads to nothing more than the good organization of the kingdom of the mediocre. Real progress requires genius. What the former contributes to the latter is only a collection of instruments and resonators.

Finally, pseudo-progress, even if it extends to all humanity, keeps its provincial horizon, while true culture goes beyond all visible reality. A heating system characterizes a time and a place, but the laws of thermodynamics belong to an intelligible order in which the universe is thought through again. The bond between the personal and the universal is a constant fact, even under the humble form of the science of natural phenomena.

When we deny to collective becoming, and even to the consciousness that we have of it, the wonderful virtues that have been so generously attributed to them since Hegel, we expose ourselves to a certain number of objections that must be considered here.

How, some people will object, can you deny that in the long line of human millennia there are privileged moments for the spirit, such as the age that saw the advent, at almost the same time and in such different places on the planet, of Zoroaster, Confucius, Buddha, Socrates and the great Jewish prophets? This coincidence cannot have been owing to chance and is scarcely explained by the influence of one of these great personalities on the others. Such an interior dynamism must be laid to the account of a bio-social force. The Spirit is at work in life.

To which we reply that great souls probably did not fail the world in other times, but the world too often failed them. If, during the first thousand years before Christ, the world was often illuminated by their action, it must be admitted that it was economically and politically more ready for them. The constitution of empires and the development of international roads offered conditions more propitious to moral freedom. But the infra-structure never engenders the super-structure; it only conditions it and gives it a system of expression, just as printing does not make men more intelligent but affords intelligent men the opportunity to make their gifts bear fruit in public and to dialogue with a greater number of other intelligent men.

It must be remembered that the inflexible formula for spiritual progress is the monologue or the dialogue, never the confused babble of the crowd. Outside the relationship of teacher to pupil and friend to friend—as distinct from that of master to slave—the transmission of values, no matter how useful, inevitably declines. When we are alone or few in number, we can make the personal order triumph in nature; but in collective mixtures the savagery of nature always ends by getting the upper hand of the personal element. This is what led Bayle to say that in politics the choice is not between the good and the bad, but between the bad and the worse.

Let us come back to our objection just noted. What is owing to the collectivity in a great millennium is not the actual advent of great souls, but their notoriety. If there have been flashes of light, it is not owing to society. On the other hand, the race, the milieu, and the moment do explain the existence of the windows which let in the light. However, their transparency is partly the result of the vigorous action of the great souls who modified the milieu. We do not have to renounce the principles laid down above: societies exercise the function of repositories or filters. They are transmitters —and subtractors.

Now let us place ourselves in the contemporary scene and consider another kind of objection. For the first time humanity is at grips with the practical problem of the unification of the planet. Is not this bio-social situation a creator of spiritual progress? Must we not be spiritualized by the *élan vital,* or perish? Nature is forcing us to choose between surpassing ourselves and annihilating ourselves. This state of things is really engendered, it would seem, by collective becoming and our awareness of it.

However, the fact is not so simple as that. First, we are the heirs of a civilization that has considerably altered our natural situation. When we admit a mechanical thrust in events, we forget all that human genius has done to lead us to our present point on the road and help us in our study of the universe. Then, there is the crucial problem of the hour—the economic unification of the world—which of itself does not bring about a spiritual uplift. It simply places us under the necessity of *choosing* values, which is not the same thing. Finally, technical perfection, and in particular the rapidity of travel and communication, while favoring the dissemination of knowledge about values or persons, also risks diminishing their inner quality. When Socrates spoke, he had about a half dozen listeners. In our day he would have millions through the press or radio. But he would also have the competition of all the crackbrains having access to a newspaper or a microphone and would have to accept the dilution of thought that often accompanies its oral expression. We say nothing of the mental confusion of the masses subjected to the incoherent jumble of ideologies. It is precisely because it is planetary in breadth that civilization is in danger of losing in depth and height.

Technical perfection is to be found in all areas, from the manipulation of things to the manipulation of minds, passing through the realm of law and politics. But everywhere it is a function with two variables: imitation and discovery, the demands of community life and the diffusion of spiritual initiative. It belongs mainly to what we called pseudo-progress, but it does not, for all that, exclude the easiest of all personal assimilations: the kind that supports an Einstein with engineers and a Bach with instrumentalists. Technical values are of a mixed nature; they perform an auxiliary task and never become absolutes. The realization of these values, especially in the material order, always has good chances of enduring, since it needs only that minimum of intelligence that prevents there being too much of it. Thus it is clear why in technology we have the only form of progress whose curve has regularly been upward for several centuries and whose decline does not even seem imaginable, now that it is possible to communicate with the whole world and perpetuate thought in print.[4] Technology is the faithful by-product of civilizations. Its future success seems to have no limits. But this success is superficial. Technology itself does not stop any more, but it does arrest the progress of spirit, communicating to it a kind of narrowness and insolence before the mystery of things. Without detesting technology, as Gabriel Marcel may do, I am in agreement with him in seeing in it a formidable power for the desacralization of things.[5]

A final variation in the doctrines of progress we have been criticizing might be expressed as follows: there is an acceleration of time in history; this is proof that the drama is drawing to a close and the mystery of groups has an absolute meaning whose sense is soon to be revealed. We agree that acceleration is certain.[6] But this can mean two very different things: either time's content is becoming more and more rich in various events, or time's rhythm is more and more rapid and so taking longer to gather the same content. Now, in both cases it is a question of quantitative variations, and not of spiritual quality. The inner enigma of collective destiny is not clarified thereby, nor the level of the drama changed.

To sum up: we do not deny that there is spiritual progress in humanity, but we do deny that it is inescapable and owing to the collective becoming. Furthermore, it cannot penetrate to the depths of human groups and find adequate expression there, since it is always more partial and precarious in proportion to the size and complexity of the group. To the history of spontaneous communities, and even communities deliberately willed by persons, we have added the only history emanating directly from the mind and capable of consoling or directing it: the succession of biographies and the analyses of centers of consciousness. In short, we judged that whereas the nineteenth century often misunderstood the mutual implications of the group and the individual in civilization, the twentieth century is carried more than once to the opposite extreme, forgetting these elements of the life of the spirit that are irreducible to the group, or those elements of the group that are refactory to the life of the spirit.[7]

Is collective becoming absurd, then, and without ultimate value? Not necessarily. One can still believe it has a spiritual destination and leads to a transcendent society in which personal spirits will gather together in perfect harmony. Nothing prevents us from even hoping that the empirical forms of this becoming already contain some traits of the final city and will be recapitulated there. Many "mystical" professions of faith follow this line of thought, from St. Augustine's *City of God,* to Karl Marx's *Capital.* But these men are mystics, inspired by faith, and not perception. They interpret the past on the basis of a future finality in history. When they claim to rely on pure facts, they take on a passionate or Utopian air. They have to apologize for the delay in the fulfillment of their prophecies, admitting that the messianic era is always postponed until tomorrow, and the present generation is always a sacrificed generation.

Whether these doctrines be Christian or atheistic, they often take advantage of the fact that collective events change color when viewed from outside and at a distance. For example, the barbarian invasion, the French Revolution, etc., seen—and above all lived—on the scale of an individual life, reek with murders, betrayals, and horrors of all kinds. If, on the contrary, we look at them several centuries later, after the ideological element has been filtered out, it is easy to convince ourselves that the Spirit spoke through these events and used them to effect transfigurations in a mystical process. The man of faith has a perfect right to think that Providence can draw good out of evil and harmonize discords. But this legitimate faith does not authorize us to declare that the path taken by the events was the only one possible, or to play the devil's game under pretext that divine ingenuity can make the devil himself work for its purposes. Unfortunately there are many sophisms sheltered under the equivocal axiom that the history of the world is the judgment of the world. Hegel, to whom we owe so many brilliant philosophical insights, misled us by inserting tyranny in his dialectic. Instead of realizing that tyranny is a bestial episode that we should regard in shame, he presents it as a spiritual episode of which we should be proud. This kind of argument has perverted every philosophy of history inspired by his.

We have just contrasted faith and perception in history. Whether faith be taken in a broad sense, or in its theological acceptation, is not a principle of this kind necessary to interpret and evaluate facts? This we do not deny, for it is indispensable even for discovering and establishing them, since events express values, and knowledge of the past is always the work of a person who receives and prolongs an earlier humanity in it. But if perception in this case implies an element of belief, this element ought to give form to the materials and not create them out of odd bits. It ought to help organize what we can know and not conjure up in fantastic fashion what we will never know. In brief, it ought to lead to discovery and not dispense from work, otherwise credulity, and not objectivity, would increase. Consequently we should distinguish many possible uses of "faith" in history; yet contemporary discussions scarcely ever bother to do so. It is legitimate to interpolate and perhaps to extrapolate, but never to extravagate.[8]

The philosopher who does not confuse his role with the

theologian's, sees collective becoming as unable to make us free. Important though the awareness of our beginnings and meanderings may be, the history of this becoming does not deliver persons from their alienation. It simply shows them the framework of their existence and the non-self inherent in their very human-ness. If this non-self is to unfold in intersubjective reciprocity, faith must go beyond facts. For my part, I can scarcely see how such a faith is possible unless it begins by affirming the action of a transcendental Being.

Even in this last perspective, the forms of social organization, particularly the national or world state, cannot be placed above persons or regarded as persons. They represent the machinery of our earthly societies, destined to disappear from a spiritual society or, at most, retain a symbolic value there. Above the gregarious soul, which is always inferior and blind, there is most certainly the effort toward civilization descending from the elite into institutions. The devotion that brings these institutions into being and the discipline they require are an introduction to the life of the spirit. But the civilizations whose jewel they are, are always intermediary and imperiled; they are partial, fragile, and still imperfect images of a rational community whose advent is not of this world, since it supposes the end and transformation of the world.[9]

NOTES

1. Grégoire clarified some aspects of the problem very well in his paper on "Hegel et la divinité de l'Etat," at the third congress of French-speaking philosophical societies held at Brussels in 1947.

2. In his *Phenomenology* Hegel has the two developments coincide

in principle "from the ancient city to the French Revolution." Nevertheless, J. Hippolyte declares that even within these limits, if it were a question of a complete philosophy of history, this would be a failure. (*Genèse et structure de la Phénoménologie de l'Esprit*, Paris, 1946, p. 41.) As for the *Philosophy of History*, the author tells us he has been obliged to forego "the pleasure of giving a detailed picture of the prosperity, the periods of glory that have distinguished the career of peoples, the beauty and grandeur of the character of individuals, and the interest attaching to their fate in weal or woe. Philosophy concerns itself only with the glory of the Idea mirroring itself in the History of the World." (Trans. by J. Sibree; New York, W. H. Allen, 1900, p. 457.) These texts need no comment.

3. Of the twenty-one civilizations Toynbee studies, he concludes that only two can be completely isolated from any other civilization, and four from any antecedent civilization. Only one seems to have escaped ruin up to this time and offers some chance for constant and direct survival: that of the West, penetrated by Christianity. See *A Study of History* (Abridgement, Oxford, 1947), p. 245 and *Civilization on Trial* (Oxford, 1948), p. 225. We may go farther than Toynbee and maintain that a certain immortality of technical values has been acquired since the Renaissance and has something of a universal character. But technology represents only the lower fringe of a true humanism and is not, properly speaking, a civilization. We will return to this point later.

4. Very close to technology is work; it, too, influences man, but more deeply than the machine with which it is associated. Despite its deplorable elements the history (and mystique) of work shows a human progress that is the highest moral limit of the collective becoming as such. It is indeed to the role of work above all that any praises offered in these paragraphs apply.

5. The most dangerous material techniques are the ones that replace the training of the subject by the purchase of a gadget. To the fascination of the object are then added alienation through money and ignorance of mechanics.

6. This is the object of an interesting sketch by D. Halévy: *L'Accélération en histoire* (Paris, 1948).

7. The development of the person is not due to the diminution of the surfaces of contact but to an original manner of utilizing and recollecting oneself in them. Nevertheless we do believe that between

private and public life there is a partial diversity of *forms,* and that not everything in the old manner of opposing them is out of date, even though it was simplistic. These forms are even antagonistic, as can be seen in our day when the systematic erasing of their frontiers is really a threat of personal dissolution.

8. See on this point the excellent warnings in H. Marrou, *De La connaissance historique* (Paris, 1956).

9. On the theological aspects of this problem I have added some reflections in the collection *Philosophies de l'histoire* (Paris, 1956), pp. 134–40.

Conclusion

13 ❖ *Toward a Personalist Synthesis*

PERSONALISM IN THE HISTORY OF PHILOSOPHY

The term personalism designates any doctrine that attributes to persons an important place in reality or, more radically, that regards them as the only reality. In a more approximative sense personalism consists in emphasizing respect for the human person in moral action and the organization of society.

There have been numerous personalist drives in history. The *gnothi se auton* of Socrates, the *autarkeia* of the Stoics, and the *societas generis humani* of Cicero suffice to show its presence and variety in the Greco-Roman world. But Christianity in particular helped enrich the idea of person, divinizing it in the dogmas of the Trinity and the Incarnation and in the concept of the Church as the Body of Christ. The Middle Ages gave a conceptual form to this notion of person and drew from it consequences of a theological, metaphysical, and moral order.[1]

Since the Renaissance, the human person has been asserting itself by occasionally cutting itself off from its religious or institutional roots; it tends, moreover, to be identified with consciousness itself, as in the *cogito* of Descartes. Thus Berkeley writes: "Nothing exists, properly speaking, except persons, i.e., conscious things. All other things are not so much beings as personal modes of being." Moral with Kant, personalism then became ontological, first with Fichte and then with Renouvier, and constituted thereafter a well-defined orientation of thought despite the diversity of forms it assumed.

The word itself, however, is recent in philosophy. It seems to have come from Germany where Spinoza's commentaries gave birth to it in a context of religious discussions. The question was to know whether the idea of an infinite personality was admissible. In 1798 Herder had spoken of God as an *"unpersönliches Wesen."* The personalists, or theists, immediately opposed the impersonalists, or pantheists. It is in this sense, for example, that Schleiermacher uses *Personalismus* in his *Reden über die Religion* and that Goethe calls Jacobi a personalist. A less special acceptation of the term does not seem to antedate Teichmüller (*Neue Grundlegung der Psychologie und Logik,* 1889). In England the word can be traced to an article appearing in 1846 in the *Quarterly Review,* but the first use of the word in a philosophical sense dates from 1865 in the *Exploratio Philosophica* of John Grote. In France, Paul Janet, under German influence, would have liked to make personalism a synonym for spiritualism, but he abandoned the idea, fearing the misunderstandings that could result, for in the French language the word would have suggested an egoistic and anarchic attitude; the same reservation still persists in Maurice Blondel. In fact it is Renouvier who is responsible for the good fortune of personalism, having succeeded in dissociating the word from all pejorative connotations (*Le Personnalisme,* 1903). Several years later, in Germany, W. Stern began to expound a "critical personalism" with pantheistic overtones (*Person und Sache,* 1906). In 1908, the American, B. P. Bowne, published a *Personalism* much closer to traditional theism.

Around 1930 there was a new move toward personalism. It was broader than the 19th century variety and distinguished by two very noticeable characteristics. On the one hand it constituted a revolt against the pressures—such as mechanization through technology and the massing of individuals into the collectivity—that contemporary civilization was bringing to bear on the individual. But on the other hand personalism was no longer the monadology it had been with Renouvier; at the outset it assumed a relation of person with other persons. These two traits can be found in Max Scheler and Nicolas Berdiaev or even, in the United States, in R. T. Flewelling. They are particularly evident in France in the posthumous work of Laberthonnière and in the *Esprit* movement founded by Emmanuel Mounier.[2]

Champion of a "personalist communitarian" revolution, Mounier fought against both liberal egoism and collective despotism. Communication was for him a first fact, but it would lose all its meaning if it did not have as a correlative a personal vocation, freedom of choice and commitment, self-formed character, and attachment to a transcendant source which places every human being above the conditioning forces of nature and society. Tension and the need to surpass oneself thus manifest a call and a grace. It is this mystical inspiration that made Mounier distrustful, in practice, of premature absolutes such as universal suffrage or group tyranny, the primacy of economics or the emancipation of politics, etc. In the same line, Jean Lacroix sees personalism as "the very intention of humanity," and studies it in its juridical and economic applications as well as in its metaphysical ones. He judges that transcendence is revealed in the immanence of history and proposes to such fraternal enemies as Marxists and existentialists that they become informed and reformed through a personalist dialectic which alone can respond to the integral energy of man and accomplish the incomplete projects of force or justice in a living intersubjective creativity. It would be easy to detect the same spirit in the work of P. Landsberg, P. Ricoeur, or Denis de Rougemont.

Less preoccupied with social problems, the philosophers that L. Lavelle and R. Le Senne grouped around the *Philosophie de l'Esprit* ordinarily refuse a specific label. But they are not far removed from the metaphysical options of Mounier, who owed so much to Gabriel Marcel and above all to J. Maritain. Finally, it may be said that at the present time there is a kind of personalism diffused among the majority of masters of the reflexive method, such as G. Madinier, G. Berger, G. Bastide, J. Nabert, Lachièze-Rey, and A. Forest, to mention only a few.[3]

Though the statements that follow do not represent an isolated view, the author claims sole responsibility for them. Based primarily on the study of the "reciprocity of centers of consciousness," it supposes that every person is a universal perspective. But these notions are more an enigma to be resolved or a program to be evaluated than simple evidence. Nothing is more difficult than to go back from the *self* to the *I* and from the *I* to the *thou,* taking into account all the varieties of species, level, and breadth that these terms imply; however, the bond that unites them is inevitable in fact and by right; it even offers, in certain respects, the initial idea that alone can support the whole personalist construct.

PHENOMENOLOGY AND THE METAPHYSICS OF PERSON

To describe the personal order is neither to explain it nor to justify it ontologically. Thus it may seem that the point of departure of personalism is ambiguous, for one does not know whether it is *a posteriori* or *a priori,* or whether it presents the philosopher's psychological experience or a general conclusion of his critical reflexions. The situation would seem to be all the more serious for a personalism of intersubjectivity than for one of the *cogito,* since it remains more dependent on perception than an reflexion; and if ambiguity disappears, is not the enterprise completely previous to a valid metaphysics?

Evil is sometimes inhibited by its excess. Such may be the case here. The thinker is not free to radically dissociate an experience so basic that it integrates and goes beyond the segmentation of methods. The relation of the *I* to the *thou* has an essential role in the being of the *I,* and the being of the *I* is inevitably affirmed in every thought. This reference, or rather this cluster of references, is such that we cannot get rid of it except by speech. Furthermore, the perception of this fundamental fact has an immediate metaphysical implication. It is doubtless necessary to distinguish between the phenomenology and the philosophy of a problem, but there always comes a time when phenomenology coincides with philosophy, were it only at the moment of the phenomenological description of the mind in the act of philosophizing. Now, the coincidence seems to us to be inevitable, not only when it is a question of the *cogito*, as Descartes showed, but also in the intentionality that unites the *cogito* with the "other"; it is so not only by title of event, but according to intelligibility itself, for no thought can be recognized as a thought without such an admission.

This position differs from Husserl's, of whom it was recently said: "He treats intersubjectivity, both in his published and in his unpublished works, more as an inevitable consequence of his concept of objectivity than as an explanation of objectivity, fact, or existence."[4] The subjective *other* is thus conceived as a possibility inherent in the constitution of the object. Even were it a necessity, for Husserl it would still remain an abstract and undetermined *other,* without causal reciprocity with the *ego.* We believe, on the contrary, that the intersubjective bond is at once concrete and thinkable and that reciprocity is influential, i.e., simultaneously given and desired from the moment it is perceived. Husserl's *thou,* like the transcendental *I,* remains suspended in the air, or at least it touches reality only through the narrow window of the conditions of objective knowledge of the logical or physical kind.

In sharp contrast with Husserl, we could not be satisfied with an existential metaphysics that would impress no reflexive transposition on the pure fact. Though philosophy may not challenge the event, it cannot dispense itself from thinking it. Descartes sounds the right note on this subject in his *Third Meditation* when, from the idea he has of himself, he extracts the notion of substance, duration, number, and other similar things; the organisms of the ideas that flow from person and symbolize it are even more numerous than he supposed and form at each moment the eternal harvest that the thinker realizes in perception. Thus the mechanical causality we project into things is only a by-product of a more refined and complex causality of which each intersubjective experience can bring us the lived nuance. We can discern its structure by an analysis that not only reaches the phenomenological essence but confers on it a metaphysical seal. We could agree, in these conditions, with Max Scheler's method and even with M. Merleau-Ponty's.

HUMAN RECIPROCITY

It is at the interhuman stage that reciprocity is the most accessible and that we first discern it. While maintaining that the relation between the *I* and *thou* is always in reality bilateral or mutual, we may, at the outset, run counter to common opinion, unaccustomed as it is to discern in persons layers any deeper than those of superficial consciousness and its dialogues. While adding that the essence of every relation between the *I* and *thou* is love, i.e., the will toward mutual promotion, we will press the paradox to the limit and dispute the validity of Sartre's thesis in which he says that "a glance cannot look at itself. As soon as I look toward the glance it disappears and all I see is eyes."[5] It is not only the reflexive power of the glance that is thus denied, but also its transitive power, with the result that each partner is walled up in himself and all intersubjectivity is set in a threatening atmosphere. Furthermore, we attribute a greater force for actualization to spiritual causality than does Gabriel Marcel for whom it remains problematical whether or not love affects the being of the other.[6]

But which love are we talking about? The phenomenologists recognize a multitude of loves. Conjugal or parental love, friendship, and devotion to a great cause, are some indication of that variety. It is not any particular one that we have in mind, but rather a genus immanent in all these species. It might seem that love of the neighbor would be broad enough to cover the idea we have in mind. But a brief analysis will suffice to show that this is not so, because it is itself a particular kind of love. Nietzsche separated it, rightly, from the love of the person farthest away, i.e., the love we bear toward a being from whom we are removed in space or time. The love of neighbor implies a perceptible encounter (even though it is not reduced to the confines of a neighborhood) and also an element of danger—sometimes undergone in common by chance (as in a trip made as a team), or willed (as in a group of mountain climbers); the danger may be located in the partner himself should one consent to be for the other a stimulating challenge or allows him a kind of salutary aggressiveness (as in the relation between patient and surgeon). Besides the responsibilities and struggles it engenders, the encounter with the other, thus understood, supposes the mediation of techniques that at one time may depersonalize the rapport (there is no longer the human contact between the railroad engineer and the passengers that there used to be between the coachman and his clients); at another time they strengthen it and make it more moving (the case of the surgeon and the communication systems that precede or accompany his decisions could be cited here). Finally, all love of the neighbor is, in the strict sense, transitory. It is a timed love, a passing episode like the one in the Gospel parable of the Good Samaritan; otherwise we would be dealing with friendship, conjugal love, or some other stable form of altruistic feeling.

Reciprocity of centers of consciousness, present in every concrete form of love, is apt to look more like an abstraction than love. Nevertheless, though it is diffracted in a series whose phenomenology examines details more often than totalities, it does correspond to an experience whose phenomenon is well founded. It is, so to speak, an essence diffused in other essences. But it must be added that before its diffraction reciprocity is the first moment in any intersubjective knowledge (for knowledge, which is always turned toward the other, is so especially in the case of intersubjectivity). For that reason it is the special experience of the nascent relationship with another concrete subject (for the first movement by which minds are approached is generous, no matter how quickly its grace may be subsequently denied). Beyond diffraction, the communion of minds is, then, a love inviting all the diffracted forces to surpass and fulfill themselves in a mutual and perfect advancement. The person, that "rational individual," is a being whose individuality is discovered and consciously developed by attaching itself to the universal so that it cannot fall back radically into its own limits without contradicting and degrading itself.

Let us first summarize the principal characteristics to be noted in interhuman reciprocity.

1. In the first place it is a *primordial factor* in the perception of persons, for the person is not known unless he some-

how gives himself to the one who looks at him. His consented presence in the world is already an act; each one receives and gives his being as soon as there is perception. And this minimum of reciprocity is thus also proportional to an initial love in which feeling, knowledge, and the will to promotion are joined together.

2. The will to promotion manifests the radical *continuity* of minds and even the heterogeneous identity of the *I* and *thou,* i.e., their community of subjects qua subjects. It introduces, of course, a cleavage in each personal center in which the ideal self is distinguished from the empirical self. But the ideal *I* communicates with the *thou* himself; and far from being dissolved in him, aims at making him exist through the same movement by which it finds its source in him. This is not to say that the destiny of the self is to be blind to what it is and what its partner is. On the contrary, the ideal self discovers selfhood purified of all that is non-self, for the ideal self does not designate the falsely idealized and imaginary self that our sentimental masks so often express; it designates the personal theme underlying all variation, good or bad, and a constant desire to be unique, each through the others. Its function is to free us, not in opposition to mutuality but through it; one of the subjects is the other in the measure that it causes the other to be. The *thou* is not a *not-I,* since it accomplishes the will of the *I* while continuing to be through itself.

3. Efficacious in its principle, reciprocity leads to a task which it accomplishes only *by stages* in the dual and laborious history of the subjects it unites. To accede to liberty as a result of an influence is not necessarily to know one's exact debt toward the other; the child is almost always ungrateful,

and gratitude is gained only by conquest. The deeper the original imprint is, the more forgetfulness of the sources seems to be the rule, as if purity and freedom with respect to the promised future demanded that provisory forgetfulness.

The education of a child or the history of a friendship shows, however, that the normal evolution of an influence involves other phases. In the act by which I am, I accept the being that I receive and immediately posit it for itself without any other reference; I assert myself with more force than finesse; and if I recognize that I have origins by the very fact that I feel I am existing, it is only in a general way, in proportion to my imperfect knowledge of myself. It often happens that one mind advances ahead of another and is mother to it without the other's having had to choose the being that constitutes it and to which it consents. But the influence is subsequently less imperious without ceasing to enrich the subject: I advance toward my causes, I try to decipher the being of my benefactor; I discuss his gifts because I live by them and make them live. Finally, between us nothing is imposed and all is proposed; or rather, everything tends to come together in a freely consented harmony and in the double pulsation of a lucid sharing in which one of the persons is no longer a late-arrival with reference to the other. Each one is called to recreate the gift he receives and the very relation that established him in his original being.

4. The development of reciprocal consciousness and the recasting of the *we* that it effects, are, however, much less complete and idyllic than the preceding schema would lead us to believe. At the interhuman level reciprocity is *always*

limited: never does it reach the depth of our beings. Doubtless there is nothing to prevent two persons from being capable of becoming entirely transparent and synergic, each with respect to the other, but never are they created by each other: they are encountered. What is more, their moments of reciprocity are rare, fragile, and interrupted by adverse currents or rival reciprocities. Besides, the human community seems restricted to a dyadic regime: it is doubtful that three or more minds can be simultaneously and equally in communion so that each one lives to the same degree with the others. But the multitude of dyads that fill the days of each personal history can, in a measure, remedy their inconstancy, by an indirect presence of all in each, thanks to an objective *we* and the common tasks it harbors.

HUMANO-DIVINE RECIPROCITY

Were we to limit ourselves to the interhuman experience of reciprocity we would have only a tattered image of the personal order—a series of dyads built up helter-skelter, without ever arriving at a substantial influence, despite the mutations that their participants operate in themselves and the universalizing rule they try to elaborate. Personalism would then be a new kind of phenomenalism. But, as we intimated, the subjects have an interior stability from another source which is transcendent. To affirm this is to introduce a humano-divine type of reciprocity quite different from interhuman reciprocity. Man is totally dependent on his creator and cannot begin on the same level with Him; his relation to God is a rather unequal mutuality, even though man is called to effect it subsequently in his turn.

What makes us take ourselves seriously is certainly not the personality that is the daughter of our works, the "unpleasant self" that Nettleship speaks of, for we are a failure to ourselves. But while detaching ourselves from ourselves, while keeping ourselves at a distance from ourselves, we still have to aim at the unique person we disclaim ever attaining or being. Now, love of the end begins by suppressing all absolute separation between phenomenon and being in the self; at the same time it forbids us to deny that at the beginning there is an absolute singularity in our perspective. To prove our personal identity it suffices to have glimpsed the possibility of transforming ourselves by gathering together all our powers and directing ourselves utterly toward totality.

The appearance of such a self and its development as a universal perspective form an outgrowth that neither the resources of nature nor the hypothetically limited and transitory influence of other created selves explain. We are thus led to find our grandeur in solitude, and that grandeur is God. It is at least the god of each intelligent being, and in addition, of each personal encounter; he alone is capable of giving them their originality and saving their continuity. I am willed by him each time I will and receive my being. I am so, by the effect of a metaphysical priority to which my fundamental self gives testimony. But this god, from whom my person springs and whose spirit wills me as such, cannot but be personal in an eminent degree. Thus, already on the human scale there is no divorce between personal and spiritual development. My own consciousness is born to the image of another Consciousness that penetrates and totally envelopes it.

On the other hand, there cannot be as many gods as human persons; polytheism is scarcely compatible with the limitless coalescence that becomes the personal god of intelligent beings. God, the only God of intelligences, cannot be cut in pieces, i.e., into attributes or separate divinities, if he is the uniqueness that takes into account all unique beings. That such a God does include super-persons in himself cannot be denied *a priori* by a personalist philosophy; quite the contrary, for there is no *I* without a *thou,* and the otherness of creation is not on an ontological level with the Creator. That is why the hypothesis of a certain personal plurality in God is plausible, independently even of the Revelation that led Athanasius to posit so clearly an eternal *genesis* above the cosmic *metousia* and thus break with the neoplatonism of the Arians.

Humano-divine reciprocity raises to the maximum degree the two constants we had discerned before; more than any other reciprocity it is both efficacious and fragile. We cannot escape the norm that establishes us in being and calls us to a universal perfection; but we can ceaselessly turn against the freedom that is communicated to us and instigate a secession or revolt. Nothing is easier than to deny God in word, both as the fruitful "beyond" of our worlds and as their most deeply immanent law, for the true God remains silent and gives himself in silence. All we have said about the pedagogical character of the degrees of interhuman reciprocity would apply here also, provided it were transposed, and provided it dissociated the humano-divine relation from the empirical forms of dialogue to which it cannot be reduced, even if it borrows them in order to surpass them.

Even for the philosopher everything happens as if God wished to be incarnated in us and we had to recreate the world in Him and with Him—a fact involving a subtle alliance of law and liberty. Such spiritual causality evidently has nothing of the instrumental about it and impels us more to infinite cooperation than to pure contemplation.

In most proofs for the existence of God we reason in virtue of a principle of causality. Our line of thought also implies recourse to the final cause of our being but does not stop at a cosmological argument. Neither have we limited ourselves to such axioms as: "The more cannot proceed from the less"—"Aseity of being contains perfection," etc., for these axioms are ambiguous and a bit too awkward; even at best they could not lead us to a God worthy of being called personal. There is certainly nothing shameful about wishing to prove God through reason and thanks to reasoning, for if He is, we cannot see why He would escape the grasp of critical thought. But reasoning in a discussion of this kind ought to sense what is unique about the case. Thus, the true proof is a proof by extraction. It shows an inevitable presence, the only one that is absolutely inevitable in every given being. The causality on which we base our argument is proper to God alone; our being designates Him as its Creator and end. This is not the way we establish the existence of an object in virtue of the logic of phenomena. We do not see everything in God, but we can perceive God in all things; and His presence that binds all together from within, safeguards a direct universality in our knowledge, although our learning is fragmentary and our human reciprocities are dyadic.

THE WORLDS OF THE IMPERSONAL

From the preceding principles certain forms of impersonality can be adduced. There is a spiritual distance separating self from self, and self from God or from the *other,* that seems inherent in the personal order of things such as we experience it in ourselves. That objectivation helps us fulfill ourselves; it is a kind of impersonality whose genesis in the bosom of the personal order is mysterious, yet represents nothing surprising or shocking. Likewise, the progressive movement through which a universe of centers of consciousness is formed and revealed to our eyes supposes an intelligible space or matter which does no violence to the mind. The evolution of beings, with its irregular rhythms, and even the eclipse of beings, may be necessary for the freedom of their development and reunion; these changes are in reality marks of God's respect for them. Another normal form of impersonality is the objectivity of knowledge. Could we not deduce the third person from the existence of the first two, in the sense that to knowledge directly addressed is substituted a report made to third parties, real or fictitious, in the absence of the one addressed? Theoretical language impoverishes intersubjective dialogue, and Dr. Lacan is correct in showing the havoc it can work, not only among the mentally ill, but even among those who wish to cure them. However, objectivity, properly understood, helps to overcome the inertias of elementary communication or rumination and becomes science or philosophy; it addresses its message to any mind and amply compensates the initial losses it inflicts on personal life.

If the world of the impersonal contained nothing else, it would not be dangerous for the personalist synthesis. It would leave us at the level of quasi angelic experience, wherein we have been moving until now in our exposition, and would scarcely extend beyond its boundaries. We have analyzed the most intrinsic data of the *cogito* and the *cogitamus* and drawn out the principal implications. There was no question in all that of abstraction or imagination, but we did not go beyond the inner layer of the mind, or at least the experiences favorable to the mind, and consider it in its perfection. In short, we simply asked that instead of saying, for example: "I am the present state of awareness, the perfume of the rose, the response to this visitor, the reflection on this idea," etc., I be disposed to say: "These states of awareness withdraw me from myself; the best thing I can do to find myself is to go through them toward myself, to link them together according to a style that symbolizes the pure and final self whose content I shall never fully achieve, but whose form unites me indefinitely to other selves in God."

Unfortunately, the impersonal has other faces than the ones just indicated; it is obstacle, contradiction, living absurdity. We first perceive it in nature, i.e., in the existence of a reality combining the non-self and the sensible. Immersed in it through the body and the vital psychism, we are estranged from our pure particular essence; nature generalizes us (which in certain respects is the contrary of universalizing us) and makes us incoherent; nevertheless it supports and prepares us, with the result that we have, in a kind of vertigo, the impression that we depend on it even for the power to be and to judge. Though we may reach beyond and escape nature, it is none the less the base from which we subtend, and when it abandons us it will cause us to die, just as it caused us to be born. It is not a pure, detachable spectacle; it is our eye, our instinct. If, beyond this disturbing *Dasein,* we observe the specific whole of humanity in which we are inserted and then the cosmic whole of infra-human beings with its disordered creativity, we must admit that the spectacle absolutely surpasses anything a personal idealism had foreseen. Nature, we insist, is more than a spectacle; it is a force that enters into our very substance. Is it necessary to stress the pathos of the situation and the violent, irrational attack the philosopher suffers as soon as he remembers he is a man and there is an earth?

Every child who is born is a part of miraculous matter in which life transfigures the molecules and consciousness will transfigure life. But this shining success does not last, does not go far, and is not explained by the individual whom it sets free. When man wills, in his turn, to exalt the world and govern its scattered forces, he never achieves it by a pure and omnipotent creation; neither will he achieve it by the miracles of the saints or the marvels of the fakirs; intellectually he descends again to the foundations and invents physical techniques by which he can ravish life and psychic nature. Such is his own triumph and the triumph he offers the earth. But matter thus glorified is ambiguous and no one yet knows whether it will not crumble into chaos and bury the creature who pierced its secret.

We have not yet come to the end of our wonders. Another world of the impersonal opens to us in the very life of the spirit insofar as the latter separates itself from other spirits and revolts against their divine norm. The demoniacal will is a depersonalization; it is in secession, while the true status of the person is collegial. If demoniacal complicity mimics spiritual society for the sake of a more refined secession, the evil is only the worse. Under this extreme form the impersonal subverts the person and tempts it with a frightening power of proliferation capable of strange and indefinitely attractive novelties.

All these facts suggest a new departure for philosophy. It can and must remain faithful to its first principles, but it cannot stop there or limit itself to them. It must squarely face the varieties of experience and abandon all hope of reasoning to a conclusion; all that remains is the possibility of inferring it in the measure that reflection can convert the obstacle into a springboard, reabsorb negative values, envision a costly salvation, and determine the conditions of an indirect victory of the personal order over the rest. But in adopting this attitude the thinker evokes another world of the impersonal: that of the enlarged anonymity that becomes the novitiate of his very personality and enriches the primary objectivity to which he was already consenting. For he must integrate the indifference or hostility of things into his "élan" and even assume in spirit the guilt and perversion of minds, converting, for example, revolt into adventure and invention; or he must simply realize that what is without finality has for its final destiny to be known as such, and thus be finalized. Far from renouncing personalism, he subsequently discovers there unsuspected regions and additional tasks. He also understands better that the person does not fulfill itself without work and that the mystique of work is tragic even in philosophy; it is a duel in which one sometimes strikes in the dark.

The neat operations of reason no longer suffice. Fine deeds, courage, and faith must be added. Nietzsche wrote, and

A. Camus repeated, that a man's energy is measured by his capacity for accepting the fundamental absurdity of the world in the name of the effort by which he organizes a fragment of it. All is not false in this far-fetched statement which proposes a desperate integration of the world in the will, if not in the mind. It is legitimate to have a north star in philosophy, but it is impossible to make a tidy philosophy in which each structure and each event could be perfectly understood and justified.

METAPHYSICAL CONSEQUENCES

1. These conditions call for a renewed effort toward a complete philosophy, a project entailing the *reorganization of categories,* bearing in mind nature to whose currents the subject must adjust before he can traverse them. Objectivity involves the exercise of categories that are valid for things and must be rethought if we apply them to subjects. Thus it will be noted that judgments concerning existence are no more homogeneous than judgments concerning attributes. The study of being, quantity, quality, etc., would show that the notions we use are often vitiated by ambiguities due to their physical origin, and consequently they cannot express subjective life without deforming it; they expose us to antinomies, omissions, and a too limited exercise of the intelligence.

Take, for example, the idea of *having,* associated with quality. It begins either with capture or with inheritance and proceeds to artificial ownership under an instrumental or juridical form. Objective having makes possible the symbolic representation of subjects, but it can immediately translate neither the deep solidarity of states of consciousness around their center nor the communion of centers of consciousness. However, possessive thought integrates with persons by allowing them to know their limits, assimilate the qualities of nature, and express what one subject operates in another subject. Can we not even maintain that reciprocity of minds is the intersection of two havings-in-the-other? At most, having becomes the work that transfigures things or ideas in the act and gives body to this act. But it does not do so unless one consents to a painful revision of its meanings and use; otherwise it ruins comprehension and is the cause of humanity's gravest ills.

2. The personalist should also leave his mark on the *theory of knowledge.* Like everyone else, he begins by reflecting on data. But from the viewpoint of the person, the datum can be an act identified with a giver (as in the experience of the *I* and *thou*), or a quasi-anonymous gift conspiring with the being of the subject (as in the case of truth values), or finally, an obstacle (as in the encounter of material or psychic exteriorities). It would be vain to try to homogenize such a variety at the outset; it would also be vain to reopen on this subject the often confused quarrel between realism and idealism. We can withdraw neither from the fact of being "embarked" in existence nor from the vocation to recreate all that characterizes our knowledge. For knowledge is not pasted on our being, it is as much a part of it as an efficacious act. Knowledge has an ontological depth and is, in a sense, necessarily altruistic, since it is turned toward something other, if not always toward another center of consciousness.

Knowledge thus bears the mark of our spontaneous or

acquired character, and this connection affects even science and philosophy, without our self-assent's necessarily impairing them. There is no contradiction between the singularity of genius and the universe it accepts or reconstructs; for thought that has the force of genius is thought in which everything is found and recognized for what it is; talent, on the other hand, is limited to a group or seeks picturesque effects. The exactitude of intelligence coincides, in this sense, with its real originality and generosity to such a degree that the more it is itself the more it becomes all things and all things become it. The danger, then, is not in being too much oneself in what one judges, but in being awkwardly and meanly so.

3. It is probably in *religious philosophy* that the repercussions of personalism are most deeply felt. We will not go back to the affirmation of God, which seems to us to be demanded by the analysis of the personal condition (contrary to what certain personalists such as W. Stern or J. E. MacTaggart have professed). We should like, rather, to indicate briefly the effects resulting in this area from the scandal of impersonal existence. The philosopher ought to be inspired with a militant, instead of a triumphal, theism.

Evil, with all its complex and disconcerting forms, drains from the human spirit all hope of defeating dualism with an adequate explanation. But it does not suppress the possibility of such an explanation. Seen from outside, our planet has, and even plainly shows, finality. It is a genesis of the more in the less; perfection is drawn from a quasi-nothingness, and a universal co-presence is achieved. But it is an unprotected finality, indifferent to the lot of individuals, furrowed by death and sin, and laden with an immense waste of spiritual energy. Only by abandoning oneself to God Himself by faith can one save the unity of experience in a meaning compatible with an infinite vocation of personal being. Only at the price of an extreme, divine ingenuity can harmony be recovered. Heraclitus declared that "God is the cause of good only"; Calvin asserted the contrary, but only in appearance, since he believed in a redemptive incarnation of the divinity. But between Heraclitus and Calvin philosophy met Christianity and partially changed its method. Since it is no longer interested only in an elite, it has had to give a larger share to a speculative faith where deduction is lacking; it lives, besides, on historical paradigms and not simply on nontemporal myths. Without being confused with a theology or an exegesis of the revealed word, it has drawn out the organisms of ideas emanating from the central figures of Christianity. On the one hand the total synthesis it seeks is eschatological, and on the other it is based on striking events which are its pledge.

Thus is explained the fact that the most noteworthy documents for religious philosophy are often personal notes and spiritual diaries, and that interest in mysticism should have continued to grow. This tendency to exalt the heroes of the interior life and draw light from contact with their exemplary personalities is philosophically legitimate. In a wider sense each one can draw certitudes about the beyond from certain privileged moments in his own life. Many human beings believe in a personal God because they have been aware of His bursting into their inner history, not as an agreeable response to their prayers, but as a meaning that gives direction to their existence, sometimes painfully and in spite of themselves. More broadly still, beauty will bear witness to the reality of a divine realm, if not of a provident God. With a force that no argument will ever equal, the music of Bach and Handel gives the conviction of crossing a frontier: such art is the irrefutable presence of an autonomous source of gracious and disinterested nobility, an absolute benignity of an order and spiritual authority about which nothing more perfect can ever be experienced or conceived. Though the reality of music is not God, it skirts his essence as it were, and causes Him to be perceived as a promised land whose existence can on longer be doubted.

Experiences of this type are not without conceptual content or communicability. They are not to be banished from philosophical research except when they are used to dispense us from the work of reflection. But a metaphysics of charity, too, should contribute to the progress of ideas. With respect to the problem of evil, it should examine, among other things, the concept of time and extract, at least as probable hypotheses, the conditions of a directiveness seen from the vantage point of the present, which makes it quite impossible for the past to appear as evil. The spiritual exigencies of thought involve a use of reversibility and irreversibility that upsets our empirical notion of "becoming" in a manner strangely parallel to what modern science has already told us. But while physics has its analysts and theorists, spiritual reality seems to lack them. The philosophy of the soul is still fallow ground.

Perhaps the reason is that we have conceived of all communication and all certitude according to physico-mathematical truth and thrust all the rest in the depths of bad subjectivity. We have thus wrongly submitted philosophical exchange to the social regulation of the content of conversation in both the private and public domain. In order to be "public," philosophy has jettisoned its best cargo. There are, however, some zones of agreement and control in the interior life and some transmissible affirmations, despite the exuberance of reality and the relatively restricted number of those whose duty it is to judge them. Finally, between doubt and certitude, which alone pleased Descartes, there is probability, which Plato did not disdain.

IMPLICATIONS FOR VALUE JUDGMENTS

1. If there is reciprocity of consciousness in love, the *I*, we said, is identified with the *thou* in the measure that it promotes it; both are thus identical and heterogeneous at the same time: a seeming contradiction. We come here to the heart of a situation inherent in every community of minds (and consequently in the very notion of reason), which poses, at the outset, a redoubtable difficulty to the logic of the excluded middle. The analysis of being and non-being ought therefore to be taken up again and pursued from the personalist point of view. If we recall, on the one hand, the expansion the categories have undergone from the fact that the person is involved in nature, we can easily understand that the criteria for the true and the false will be complex. But it is impossible to limit oneself, outside the impersonal, to the norms of the impersonal alone. To the conditional connections that mathematical logic inventories with the help of what might be called the imagination of the objective understanding, there is added a series of properties and measurements of another type: norms anterior to the individual himself and his acts, affinities that combine or

disperse the traits of character, sequences of a history or a group—in short, the whole logic of concrete development, one of the main segments of which is the convergence of probabilities. Logic is always formal; but for human experience the logic one usually has in mind would be only a science of poor or displaced forms.

2. *Esthetics* extends into metaphysics: salvation by way of aesthetics is one way out of the problem of evil. Thus, a theory of art that assigned no other role to the work of art than to exhibit the psychic character of the artist would be a very superficial one. Art has more and better things to do: it is the creation of a quasi-person in the work itself; it is demiurgic; it rivals nature; it aims at an immediate individuation of materials and sheds an autonomous meaning in every organism they form. But this creation never completely passes from essence to existence. The survival of the work supposes at least the active presence of the spectator. That is why there also subsists an element of illusion in art, just as there subsists in every value an element of distance with reference to the person from whom it emanates, though he be divine.

Each art is based on the predominance of a sense organ. As for the hierarchy of the arts, it would seem to respond less to the intrinsic dignity of a sense than to the possibility of introducing a personal organization in an act, i.e., an insertion of the universal in the particular and a passage from having to being. The effect of this is to condemn the composite arts (opera, sound films) to a subordinate position.

3. The tie between personalism and *ethics* is very close, and no one will give the lie to Kant on this point. But the

danger of becoming nothing but systems of morality menaces even the philosophies of person.

How is moral growth to be conceived? In discontinuity or in continuity? The two perspectives may appear at first to be equally valid: a systematic flight that forgets the past and goes forward, or, contrariwise, a kind of integral conservatism that insists on repeating the first lived moment of existence. In any case, these extreme and partial positions do not satisfy the thirst for fidelity found in the essence of moral life. True fidelity is a directed adventure, a logic of the self achieved through living and ever temporary images, since it must respond by the affirmation of self to the grace of a universal vocation. Fidelity is a thrust and a summons; beyond this, it formulates its own maxims for action, choosing among the natural qualities available to it, the qualities expressive of the personal conscience. Ethics is ultimately only the logic of the person who must possess himself to give himself. But this is a logic of invention and not only of result, a logic of the entire subject and not simply of knowledge or of object. It constantly combines the light of aspirations, action in progress, and completed acts. The precepts it adopts result from this multiple dialectic and the propositions it weaves.

To be faithful one must be oneself; to be oneself one must be at least two, and to be fully oneself, the other must be God. Thus fidelity is also bound to a reciprocity of centers of consciousness. It is not built outside the initiatives of the self nor by discarding messages received from other beings. The image we fashion of our fidelity would not be correctly drawn if we did not consider the expectations of the other, i.e., the idea he has of our consistance and of his own—in the *Dasein* that has fallen to our lot and in the center of the natural or institutional cadres that sustain us all. Moral phenomenology, with all its complications and conflicts, brings us back to an ontology of the person and opens out on a metaphysics of charity, since on the other hand the will that is truly good becomes pharisaical as soon as it isolates itself, and on the other it ends by deciphering in the enigma of conduct something quite different from a rule of conduct, especially when faced with the drama of infidelity and sin.

4. Must we ultimately speak of *political and social corollaries* in personalism? We are very reluctant to do so. It doubtless has an affinity for the spirit of federation, and citizens animated with such an ideal ought to reject, in the parties to which they adhere, solutions that call for tyranny or the leveling of classes. But the better part of wisdom is not to expect too much from collective life, for it is too close to the convulsive moments of nature not to be struck with spiritual indigence. It preserves or transmits certain personal initiatives thanks to which a civilization is painfully built; but it degrades them too often without ever replacing or creating them. It is true that the illusion of being able to model society at the pleasure of the human will in the short space of a generation is very tenacious in man; but it is no less an illusion for all that.

Though personalism cannot patronize any party, it can arouse a spirit of cooperation between individuals who function in a given economic or social organization. In *L'Usine sans âme* (*The Soulless Factory*) that H. Lespès recently denounced, and which is the image of modern collectivism of exaggerated size, such individualities can little by little substitute for the relation of master and slave more valid relations, such as that of teacher and disciple, knight and squire, etc. It belongs to the sociologists to open the way to the progress which can thus be accomplished, or else record it, inspired by the microsociology of Gurvitch or the analyses of Mead and Moreno. This is not, however, to expect salvation to burst from an easy formula or a pernicious romanticism. Improvements come only slowly, passing through the law of sacrifice and temporary failure, without dispensing love from being just or from organizing technically the life of the community. The personalist spirit consists in constantly discovering the modes of acting whereby the action of man on things is no longer opposed to the advancement of man by man. The urgent task is to work toward this discovery, instead of yielding to the intoxication of technology or fleeing from it by rejecting the most powerful tools of the human organism. Then it is necessary—and this is still more difficult—to see that the advancement of one man helps other men and does not impel him toward disdainful superiority or general mediocrity, or worse still, tempt him to seek refuge in a one-man ghetto to escape from the problems of all.

In certain respects personalism desacralizes nature and society, but only up to a point, for it aims at giving them value by transfiguring the physical patterns of our environment, by ordering them to our ends, and finally, by creating in the spontaneous solidarity of the species a moral society that will sometimes be the inverse of spontaneous, for its new structures will be our work. This kind of movement is never finished, but it is always worth beginning anew.

Let us add a final reflection. As long as there are philosophers there will be talk of cause, substance, and end. But these notions, discredited by an already outworn physicism, are undergoing a crisis today and must be rethought. Meditation on the person and the bond between persons stimulates this kind of thinking more than anything else. The study of this bond has been neglected until recent years; it offers to phenomenologists and metaphysicians alike a field of observation and reflection that is still but little explored.

Progress in philosophy is not achieved by the radical abandonment of the past, but by a spiral return to notions that remain imperfect and perfectible and, for this very reason, durable. In this perpetual reform, which often makes the spirit pass through the trial of negation, concern for exactitude will always be necessary. The era of closed systems is past; the more recent fashion favoring shouts and stammerings will pass too, for philosophy is not rhetoric. Personalism offers philosophers a more valid method, since its development depends on an effort to reconcile existential teachings and the exigencies of reason. It obliges us to attempt this osmosis on two levels: first, by following through to the direct implications of the personal order; and second, by facing the universe of the impersonal with physical courage and intellectual daring.[7]

NOTES

1. For E. Gilson, personalism characterizes the philosophy of the Middle Ages. See *The Spirit of Medieval Philosophy,* trans., A. H. C. Downes (New York, 1936), chap. x. The scholastics wrote many commentaries on Boethius' celebrated definition of person. I have tried to extract the ideas of this thinker on the question, in an article

on "Les Variations de Boèce sur la personne," *Revue des Sciences Religieuses,* XXIX (1955), pp. 201–38.

2. For a good introduction to the thought of Emmanuel Mounier, see his *Be Not Afraid* (New York, Sheed and Ward, 1962).

3. To complete this summary guide, the reader might refer to the note "Je et tu," drawn up with J. Pucelle for Lalande's *Vocabulaire philosophique* (7th ed.). He might also read J. Pucelle's fine work, *La Source des valeurs* (Paris, 1957) I, "Les relations intersubjectives."

4. Q. Lauer, *Phénoménologie de Husserl* (Paris, 1955), p. 49. The most elaborate demonstration of this was given in an yet unpublished paper by the late A. Schutz, "L'intersubjectivé d'après Husserl," at the Easter 1957 study days at Royaumont. See also by the same author *Collected Papers* (The Hague, 1962), Vol. I, pp. 194–197 and pp. 294–297.

5. *Being and Nothingness,* p. 268.

6. Gabriel Marcel, *Journal métaphysique* (Paris, 1927). English translation by Bernard Wall, *Metaphysical Journal* (Chicago, Regnery, 1952), p. 223.

7. The program we have outlined is not limitative. A philosophy of the person is not without influence on law, medicine, educational psychology, etc. We meet some difficult problems there and should not be satisfied with clichés.